Series / Number 07-020

LOG-LINEAR
MODELS

DAVID KNOKE
PETER J. BURKE
Indiana University

SAGE PUBLICATIONS
The International Professional Publishers
Newbury Park   London   New Delhi

SAGE Publications, Inc.
2455 Teller Road
Newbury Park, California 91320

SAGE Publications Ltd.
6 Bonhill Street
London EC2A 4PU
United Kingdom

SAGE Publications India Pvt. Ltd.
M-32 Market
Greater Kailash I
New Delhi 110 048 India

International Standard Book Number 0-8039-1492-X

Library of Congress Catalog Card No. L.C. 80-17031

95 96 97 **98** 99 20 19 18 17 16 15

When citing a professional paper, please use the proper form. Remember to cite the correct
Sage University Paper series title and include the paper number. One of the two following
formats can be adapted (depending on the style manual used):

(1) IVERSEN, GUDMUND R. and NORPOTH, HELMUT (1976) "Analysis of Variance." Sage University Paper series on Quantitative Applications in the Social Sciences,
07-001. Beverly Hills and London: Sage Pubns.

OR

(2) Iversen, Gudmund R. and Norpoth, Helmut. 1976. *Analysis of Variance.* Sage University Paper series on Quantitative Applications in the Social Sciences, series no. 07-001.
Beverly Hills and London: Sage Publications.

CONTENTS

Editor's Introduction

By writing LOG-LINEAR MODELS, David Knoke and Peter J. Burke have done us all a favor. In most fields of social science research, the last several years have seen a burgeoning number of articles which rely on various techniques for the multivariate analysis of categoric, or nominal level, data. Yet most practicing social scientists have been confused by these new techniques, since the terminology is generally unfamiliar and seemingly unrelated to the concepts involved in the more commonly understood methods of correlation and regression analysis. If you are befuddled by articles which toss around terms such as odds ratios, marginal and conditional odds, the general log-linear model, saturated or unsaturated models, effect parameters, and the like, you have come at last to the right place. Knoke and Burke begin at the beginning and introduce, define, discuss, and give numerous examples to clarify the meaning of these terms, and in the process, they render these mysterious concepts comprehensible to even the most uninitiated novice.

Knoke and Burke discuss the general log-linear model, which makes no distinctions between independent and dependent variables, but is used to examine relationships among categoric variables by analyzing expected cell frequencies; they also discuss the logit model, which examines the relationships between dependent and independent variables by analyzing the expected odds of a dependent variable as a function of independent variables. They initiate the discussion by working only with dichotomous variables and then build to a treatment of polytomous variables.

LOG-LINEAR MODELS is replete with substantive examples, most of which are drawn from political sociology. Extended examples in this paper include the relationship between voluntary association membership and voting turnout, controlling for race and education; a causal analysis of the demographic determinants of civil liberties attitudes among the United States public; a comparative cross-sectional analysis of the relationship between party identification and vote for President in 1972 and 1976; an examination of the relationship between party identification and religion in a panel study between 1956 and 1960; an analysis of the relationship between religion and attitude toward abortion; an examination of intergenerational occupational mobility; and several additional examples. Each example illustrates specific uses of log-linear models, such as their use as causal modelling analogues; their use to conduct time series analyses; their use to examine simultaneously the effect of several categorical independent variables on a categorical dependent variable; and so on. The reader will not only begin to understand the basic concepts involved in specifying and testing log-linear models but will also develop a good sense of their wide range of applications because of Knoke and Burke's generous use of examples involving many different data sets. Clearly, the range of applications is even wider, and although the use of log-linear models has perhaps "caught on" to the greatest extent in Sociology in recent years, no doubt it will become a more important tool in Political Science, Economics, Anthropology, Mass Communications, and other fields during the next decade. It may even make well-deserved inroads on analysis of variance techniques in Psychology and Educational Testing.

Although Knoke and Burke are obvious enthusiasts and hope not only to explicate log-linear modelling but to promote it, they do recognize some of its shortcomings and cover some special problems related to applications of these modelling techniques to less than tidy substantive problems. They conclude their presentation with a nice section in which they examine special problems in applying log-linear models, problems that anyone who hopes to use them effectively must face.

I fully expect that even though some of the material is difficult and requires careful study, particularly for the statistical novice, the clarity with which Knoke and Burke have written this paper will make it widely accessible. This presentation is among the best pedagogic treatments of log-linear models, a very difficult topic to explicate clearly.

—John L. Sullivan, Series Editor

During the past decade a revolution in contingency table analysis has swept through the social sciences, casting aside most of the older forms for determining relationships among variables measured at discrete levels. Through the work of Mosteller, Goodman, Bishop, and others, these new techniques have been given a solid foundation in theoretical statistics. With the availability of computer programs to perform the necessary calculations, these new models have increasingly proliferated in substantive applications to social science data problems. Yet the methods are sufficiently recent and seemingly so dissimilar to more familiar techniques that a nontechnical introduction to the topic is warranted.

In this paper we shall deal primarily with hierarchical log-linear models for multiway crosstabulations. Although log-linear models, particularly in their most general form, often strike people as a radically new development, a closer study reveals many similarities with ordinary regression. Since multiple regression—in which one variable is taken as the linear function of the values of several independent variables—is a more widely known method, we shall draw explicit parallels between it and log-linear modelling. Regression procedures are normally used to predict numerical values only on an interval or ratio scale dependent variable. However, when the dependent variable is a dichotomy, coded "1" if, for example, respondents agree and "0" if respondents disagree with a survey item, then an ordinary regression upon predictor variables can be interpreted as showing how the *probability* of a favorable response is affected. In one

AUTHORS' NOTE: *For their valuable comments on an earlier draft we thank James A. Davis, Lowell Hargens, Elton F. Jackson, William M. Mason, Richard Niemi, Susan R. Schooler, John L. Sullivan, and Karl Schuessler.*

7

major version of log-linear models, a dichotomous dependent variable can be treated analogously to a regression, with the essential difference that the independent variables affect not the probability but the *odds* on the dependent variable (e.g., the ratio of favorable to unfavorable responses). Other similarities between regression and log-linear models will be pointed out as we go along. Some similarities to probit analysis also may be seen, although we shall not develop them in this paper.

1. RELATIONSHIPS IN CROSSTABULATIONS

We shall present the basic principles of log-linear methods through a detailed analysis of the relationship between voluntary association membership and voting turnout. The substantive problem comes from the political sociology of democratic participation. For many years researchers have known that persons belonging to voluntary organizations are more likely to engage in a variety of political activities such as contacting public officials about community problems, campaigning for candidates, and voting in elections (Verba and Nie, 1972; Olsen, 1972). Some question remains whether this association is a spurious consequence of social status, which is positively correlated with both variables, and whether blacks and whites differ in their political activism once associational involvement and social status are controlled (see Thomson and Knoke, 1980).

To analyze these hypotheses, we chose data from the 1977 General Social Survey, a national sample of 1530 noninstitutionalized adults (18 years and over) conducted annually (now biennially) by the National Opinion Research Center in Chicago under the direction of James A. Davis with funding from the National Science Foundation. Voting Turnout (V) is the respondent's report of whether he or she voted in the 1976 election (ineligibles were omitted). Membership in voluntary organizations (M) is the count of the number of associations in a list of 16 types to which the respondent belongs, leaving out membership in churches (see Knoke and Thomson, 1977, for a discussion of how church membership differs from other types). We contrast those persons belonging to no organizations with those having one or more memberships. Race (R) is also a dichotomy, between whites and nonwhites (mostly black). Finally, education (E) was recoded into three major categories: less than high school graduation; high school graduation; some college experience including graduation or more. Ultimately we shall analyze relationships in this full four-way crosstabulation, but initially we concentrate on the membership-vote turnout relationship, conceptualizing the latter variable as dependent or contingent upon the other. Later examples will treat multicategory variables and the dangers in collapsing to fewer categories.

The traditional way to identify a relationship, or association, between two categoric variables is to calculate percentages within categories of the independent variable and to compare these percentages across the categories of the independent variable. If the percentages differ by a significant amount (using the usual chi-square test for independence) between or among the categories, an association is said to exist. The form of the association—monotonic, linear, or nonlinear—depends upon the pattern of percentages within the cells of the table (Reynolds, 1977). In Table 1, 54% of persons with no memberships voted while 75% of those belonging to one or more memberships voted. Voting turnout increased 21 percentage points among those with memberships over those without memberships in voluntary associations. Chi-square for this table is 67.7, indicating a statistically significant association (p < .001) between those variables.

In order to use log-linear models, we must first reconceptualize the dependent variable. Instead of a proportion—where the cell frequency is divided by the category total—an *odds* is the basic form of the variation to be explained. We are most familiar in everyday life with odds from horse racing and other forms of gambling. An odds is the ratio between the frequency of being in one category and the frequency of not being in that category. Its interpretation is the chance that an individual selected at random will be observed to fall into the category of interest rather than into another category. For example, in Table 1, the odds that a person voted in the 1976 presidential election are 987/486 = 2.03, or about two-to-one. (Note that some self-reported inflation seems to be going on here, since the actual turnout was about 55% of the potential voters, an odds of only 1.22.)

The odds just calculated is a *marginal odds*, applying to the total frequencies in one margin of the table without regard to the effects of any other variable. We can also calculate the *conditional odds* within the body of the table, corresponding to the traditional percentages. Conditional odds are the chances of voting relative to nonvoting given a particular

TABLE 1

Crosstabulation of Vote Turnout and Organizational Membership

		Membership (M)		
		One or More	None	Total
Vote Turnout (V)	Voted	$f_{11} = 689$	$f_{12} = 298$	$f_{1.} = 987$
	Not Voted	$f_{21} = 232$	$f_{22} = 254$	$f_{2.} = 486$
	Total	$f_{.1} = 921$	$f_{.2} = 552$	$f_{..} = 1473$

level of organizational membership. For Table 1, the odds on voting are 1.17 among nonmembers and 2.97 among members. Thus, the odds on voting are more than 2.5 times greater among association members than among persons belonging to no group.

Notice that if one of the "not voted" cells had no frequency, the odds would be undefined since an integer cannot be meaningfully divided by zero. For this reason, many analysts in the past routinely added one-half (.5) to each cell entry before performing a log-linear analysis. The advisability of this practice is questionable, and our data will not require any such adjustments in this paper.

In a traditional percentage table, two variables are unrelated if the percentages are identical or very close across all leves of the independent variable. Similarly, in an odds table, the variables are unassociated if all the conditional odds are equal or close to each other, and hence equal to the marginal odds as well. Substantively, the chances that a person voted would be the same whatever his or her social participation.

To compare directly two conditional odds, a single summary statistic can be formed by dividing the first conditional odds by the second, forming an *odds ratio*. The odds ratio is the workhorse of log-linear models, so it behooves us to spend some time exploring its features and interpretations. To see what an odds ratio does, start with the orginal frequencies forming the two conditional odds:

$$\text{observed odds ration (VM)} = (f_{11}/f_{21})/(f_{12}/f_{22})$$

which upon simplification becomes the familiar crossproduct ratio for a 2 × 2 table:

$$\text{odds ratio (VM)} = (f_{11})(f_{22})/(f_{21})(f_{12}).$$

Note that a traditional measure of association for 2×2 tables, Yule's Q, is a simple function of the odds ratio:

$$\text{Yule's Q} = \frac{\text{odds ratio} - 1}{\text{odds ratio} + 1} = \frac{(f_{11})(f_{22}) - (f_{12})(f_{21})}{(f_{11})(f_{22}) + (f_{12})(f_{21})}.$$

While Yule's Q ranges in value from -1.00 to $+1.00$, with zero indicating no relationship, odds ratios take only positive values, have no upper limit, and are 1.00 when no relationship exists (i.e., the two conditional odds are equal). Odds ratios larger than 1.00 indicate direct covariation between variables, while odds ratios smaller than 1.00 indicate an inverse relationship. Of course, "direction" of covariation is arbitrary when the variables are measured only at the nominal level since category order can be changed. In our example, voting and belonging to organizations are considered "higher" values than not voting or not belonging. Hence, the observed odds ratio (VM) of 2.53 means a positive relationship, with the odds on voting among persons belonging to organizations more than 2.5 times greater than the voting odds among those respondents without memberships.

2. THE LOG-LINEAR MODEL

A. Specifying Models

A model, in the sense we use the term, is a statement of the expected cell frequencies of a crosstabulation (F_{ij}'s) as functions of parameters representing characteristics of the categorical variables and their relationships with each other. The parameters are related to the odds and odds ratios, discussed above, as we will elaborate shortly. In assessing how well a model "explains" or fits the data, we are concerned with the extent to which the frequencies expected under the model (the F_{ij}'s) approximate the frequencies actually observed (the f_{ij}'s). In Chapter 3 we consider how to evaluate the fit of the model to the data, but first we must develop some notation and techniques for generating the expected frequencies.

There are two major approaches to log-linear modelling of contingency table data. (1) The *general log-linear model* does not distinguish between independent and dependent variables. All variables are treated alike as "response variables" whose mutual associations are explored. Under the general log-linear model, the criteria to be analyzed are the expected cell frequencies, F_{ij}'s, as a function of all the variables in a model. We will develop this approach first since it provides a basis for the second. (2) In the *logit model* one variable is chosen as the dependent variable. The criterion to be analyzed is the expected odds (Ω_{ij}) (omega) as a function of the other, independent variables. The logit model is closely analogous to ordinary regression. Elaboration of this approach must await explication of the general log-linear model. By extension it is possible to choose two variables as dependent and to analyze the relationship between them as a function of other variables.

Saturated models. We begin our discussion of models by presenting one possible model for a 2 × 2 crosstabulation such as in Table 1. This model is known as a saturated model because all possible effect parameters are present in the model. It has the form

$$F_{ij} = \eta \tau_i^V \tau_j^m \tau_{ij}^{VM}. \qquad [1]$$

The F_{ij} represents the number or frequency of cases in cell i, j which are expected to be present if the model is true. The η (eta) is the geometric mean of the number of cases in each cell in the table and is a term which is much like the intercept term in a regression equation. It is a baseline or starting point from which effects are measured and usually has no substantive meaning in and of itself. The τ (tau) terms each represent "effects" which the variables have on the cell frequencies. These effect parameters are related to the odds and odds ratio discussed above. The τ_i^V effects (one for each of the i levels of V) are present if the distribution on the vote variable across categories of the membership variable is unequal (non-rectangular) on the average. The τ_j^M effects (one for each of the j categories of M) are present if the distribution on the membership variable across categories of the vote variable is unequal (non-rectangular) on the average. Finally, the τ_{ij}^{VM} effects (one for each of the ij cells of the table) are present to the extent that turnout and membership are not independent (i.e., are associated). Given these nine effect parameters, the four expected cell frequencies of Table 1 can be represented by the model as shown in Table 2.

Note that in this model (as in all log-linear models) cell frequencies (or expected cell frequencies) are represented as the product of a series of terms. Aside from the eta term representing an average or baseline cell frequency, the magnitude of an effect is measured as a departure from the value of 1.00. Effects of exactly 1.00 have no impact since they leave the product unchanged. If there were no effects, then each cell frequency would be equal to each other cell frequency and all would be equal to the value of the eta term. To the extent that an effect parameter is greater than 1.00, there will be more than the average number of cases expected in that cell, while if the tau parameters are less than 1.00, there will be fewer than the average number of cases expected in that cell.

TABLE 2
Expected Cell Frequencies for Saturated Model

		Membership (M)	
		One or More	None
Vote Turnout (V)	Voted	$F_{11} = \eta \tau_1^V \tau_1^M \tau_{11}^{VM}$	$F_{12} = \eta \tau_1^V \tau_2^M \tau_{12}^{VM}$
	Not Voted	$F_{21} = \eta \tau_2^V \tau_1^M \tau_{21}^{VM}$	$F_{22} = \eta \tau_2^V \tau_2^M \tau_{22}^{VM}$

For dichotomous variables, such as membership and voting turnout, the tau effect parameters for each variable's categories are reciprocals:

$$\tau^V = \tau_1^V = 1/\tau_2^V \qquad [2]$$

$$\tau^M = \tau_1^M = 1/\tau_2^M. \qquad [3]$$

The numerical subscripts on each tau refer to the category of the variable to which the tau value applies. Thus τ_1^V is the effect on the expected cell frequency of being in the first category of voting turnout ("voted"), while its reciprocal τ_2^V is the effect of being in the second turnout category ("not voted"). The constraints in Equations 2 and 3 ensure that the product of the τ^V for both levels of the vote and the product of the τ^M for both levels of membership each equal 1.00. Similarly, the four τ^{VM} have the following three constraints so that their joint product is also 1.00:

$$\tau^{VM} = \tau_{11}^{VM} = \tau_{22}^{VM} = 1/\tau_{12}^{VM} = 1/\tau_{21}^{VM}. \qquad [4]$$

Since there are more effect parameters (9) than cell frequencies (4), the saturated model could not be estimated without the five constraints (Equations 1 to 4) described above. These constraints mean that only four effect parameters are independent (one for η, V, M, and VM). With four independent effect parameters and four cells in the table, the saturated model will perfectly reproduce the observed cell frequencies with no degrees of freedom remaining. (Degrees of freedom for testing models are discussed below. In general, the number of taus set equal to 1.00 determine the degrees of freedom.) We may therefore treat the observed f_{ij}'s as identical to the expected F_{ij}'s in a saturated model for any contingency table. When we specify other models which require fewer effect parameters than the number of cells in the contingency table to estimate the expected cell frequencies, we pick up degrees of freedom with which to test the goodness of fit between the modelled data and the observed data.

Using the equations in Table 2, we can derive formulae to represent the tau-effect parameters in terms of the (expected) cell frequencies. In this way, what the effect parameters represent can be made clearer. To interpret the effect parameters for the vote-membership association, we use the expected odds ratio described earlier:

$$\Omega^{VM} = \text{expected odds ratio (VM)} = \frac{F_{11}\,F_{22}}{F_{21}\,F_{12}} = \frac{F_{11}/F_{21}}{F_{12}/F_{22}} \quad [5]$$

which we previously found to be 2.531 (since observed and expected frequencies are identical in a saturated model). Next, substitute for the four F_{ij}'s the four equations found in Table 2 and simplify:

$$\frac{F_{11}\,F_{22}}{F_{21}\,F_{12}} = \frac{(\eta\,\tau_1^V\,\tau_1^M\,\tau_{11}^{VM})\,(\eta\,\tau_2^V\,\tau_2^M\,\tau_{22}^{VM})}{(\eta\,\tau_2^V\,\tau_1^M\,\tau_{21}^{VM})\,(\eta\,\tau_1^V\,\tau_2^M\,\tau_{12}^{VM})} = \frac{\tau_{11}^{VM}\,\tau_{22}^{VM}}{\tau_{21}^{VM}\,\tau_{12}^{VM}}. \quad [6]$$

This relationship shows that the odds ratio depends only on the magnitude and direction of the association between V and M and not on the marginal distributions of the variables. Using the identities in Equation 4, we can rewrite this odds ratio in terms of a function of a single two-variable parameter:

$$F_{11}\,F_{22}/F_{21}\,F_{12} = [\tau^{VM}]^4 \quad [7]$$

or

$$\tau^{VM} = (F_{11}\,F_{22}/F_{21}\,F_{12})^{1/4}. \quad [8]$$

Thus the parameter for the vote-membership covariation is the fourth root of the crossproduct ratio—the odds ratio—of the expected frequencies under the model. In the illustration, this value is 1.261.

Turning next to the single-variable tau parameters, τ_i^V and τ_j^M, and following the same steps as above, we can arrive at a representation for those terms. We begin with a product of two conditional odds

$$\left(\frac{F_{11}}{F_{21}}\right)\left(\frac{F_{12}}{F_{22}}\right) = \left(\frac{\eta\,\tau_1^V\,\tau_1^M\,\tau_{11}^{VM}}{\eta\,\tau_2^V\,\tau_1^M\,\tau_{21}^{VM}}\right)\left(\frac{\eta\,\tau_1^V\,\tau_2^M\,\tau_{12}^{VM}}{\eta\,\tau_2^V\,\tau_2^M\,\tau_{22}^{VM}}\right)$$

$$= \left(\frac{\tau_1^V\,\tau_{11}^{VM}}{\tau_2^V\,\tau_{21}^{VM}}\right)\left(\frac{\tau_1^V\,\tau_{12}^{VM}}{\tau_2^V\,\tau_{22}^{VM}}\right) = \frac{\left(\tau_1^V\right)^2}{\left(\tau_2^V\right)^2} = (\tau^V)^4$$

or

$$\tau^V = (F_{11}\,F_{12}/F_{21}\,F_{22})^{\frac{1}{4}}$$

similarly

$$\tau^M = (F_{11}\,F_{21}/F_{12}\,F_{22})^{\frac{1}{4}}.$$

An alternative representation which yields further insight into the meaning of the tau parameters can be obtained by multiplying the two preceding equations by $(F_{11}F_{12}/F_{11}F_{12})^{\frac{1}{4}}$ for V and by $(F_{11}F_{21}/F_{11}F_{21})^{\frac{1}{4}}$ for M. This exercise shows that tau coefficients represent the ratio of the number of expected cases in one category to the geometric average of the expected cases in all categories of the crosstabulation. Thus,

$$\tau_i^V = \frac{(F_{i1}\,F_{i2})^{\frac{1}{2}}}{(F_{11}\,F_{12}\,F_{21}\,F_{22})^{\frac{1}{4}}} \qquad [9]$$

or

$$\tau_j^M = \frac{(F_{1j} \, F_{2j})^{1/2}}{(F_{11} \, F_{12} \, F_{21} \, F_{22})^{1/4}} \cdot \qquad [10]$$

The formulations again ensure that the products of the taus for a variable will equal 1.00. The more that a tau effect departs from 1.00, the farther that marginal category falls from having 1/K the sample cases, where K is the number of categories for a variable (K = 2 for dichotomies). In other words, the single-variable taus reflect the amount of skewness of cases across the variable's categories.

Finally, by similar procedures the constant, η, in each equation of the expected cell frequencies is simply the geometric mean of all the (expected) cell frequencies. (Geometric means are the nth root of the product of n numbers.) Since there are four cells in our 2×2 example table, the value of η is the fourth root of the product of the four expected cell frequencies. Because in the saturated model the expected cell frequencies are identical to the observed cell frequencies, we can now calculate all parameter estimates:

$$\hat{\eta} = (f_{11} \, f_{12} \, f_{21} \, f_{22})^{1/4} = 331.657$$

$$\tau_1^V = \frac{1}{\tau_2^V} = \frac{(f_{11} \, f_{12})^{1/2}}{\hat{\eta}} = 1.366$$

$$\tau_1^M = \frac{1}{\tau_2^M} = \frac{(f_{11} \, f_{21})^{1/2}}{\hat{\eta}} = 1.205$$

$$\tau_{11}^{VM} = \tau_{22}^{VM} = \frac{1}{\tau_{12}^{VM}} = \frac{1}{\tau_{21}^{VM}} = \left(\frac{f_{11} \, f_{22}}{f_{21} \, f_{12}}\right)^{1/4} = 1.261.$$

Using these estimates (without rounding), we can exactly reproduce the four cell frequencies:

$$F_{11} = (331.657)(1.366)(1.205)(1.261) = 689$$
$$F_{12} = (331.657)(1.366)(1/1.205)(1/1.261) = 298$$

$$F_{21} = (331.657)(1/1.366)(1.205)(1/1.261) = 232$$
$$F_{22} = (331.657)(1/1.366)(1/1.205)(1.261) = 254.$$

A closer look at these estimates is in order before proceeding to nonsaturated models for the 2×2 table. The τ^V parameter stands for the square root geometric mean of the two conditional odds on voting. In this case the average conditional odds are somewhat better than even (greater than 1:1) that a person drawn randomly from the sample will have voted in 1976. Note that this conditional odds is not the same as the unconditional odds of 2.03 which were calculated from the marginal row totals. Conditional odds take into account the distributions of cases across the other variables in the table, while the marginal (unconditional) odds do not reflect the presence of other factors in the data. The effect of τ^M is greater than 1.00, showing that on average more people belong to at least one association than do not belong to any organization. Finally, the τ^{VM} stands for the odds of voting given that one belongs to some associations relative to the odds of voting given that one belongs to no associations. (Alternatively, this effect and its companion odds ratio can be viewed as the odds of belonging to organizations given that one has voted. Under the general log-linear model, neither variable is considered dependent on the other. Thus, either interpretation is legitimate. Looking ahead, however, we shall later view voting turnout as an outcome contingent on the other variables.)

Nonsaturated models. A saturated model represents the cell frequencies of a crosstabulation as a function of effects for the general mean (η), each variable, and their interrelationships. But a saturated model has no parsimony since it represents C cells with exactly C effects. The expected frequencies from a saturated model always perfectly match the observed frequencies. More parsimonious and simpler models can be constructed by setting some of the effect parameters to 1.00, which is analogous in regression to a priori designating a regression coefficient to equal zero (i.e., assuming that a particular variable has no effect on the dependent variable). Such nonsaturated models generally provide expected frequencies more or less discrepant from the observed data. The next section considers how to evaluate the fit of the model to the data.

Among the several nonsaturated models for the data in Table 1 is one in which the two-variable parameters have been set to 1.00 (setting one $\tau_{ij}^{VM} = 1.00$ automatically sets the other three to 1.00 because of the constraints imposed). This model is one in which voting turnout and organizational membership are assumed unrelated in the sense that is tested by the traditional chi-square test for independence in a two-way table. The expected cell frequencies under this model are:

$$F_{ij} = \eta \, \tau_i^V \, \tau_j^M. \tag{11}$$

Additional models with other taus set to 1.00 include:

$$F_{ij} = \eta \, \tau_i^V \tag{12}$$

$$F_{ij} = \eta \, \tau_j^M \tag{13}$$

$$F_{ij} = \eta \tag{14}$$

The five models given in Equations 1 and 11 to 14 are the entire set necessary to test a variety of hypotheses about the relationships among the two variables in Table 1. Notice that no model contains a higher order tau (e.g., τ^{VM}) without also containing the lower order taus embedded in it (e.g., τ^V and τ^M). This hierarchical feature of log-linear analysis will be discussed more fully below and procedures permitting the testing of non-hierarchical models will be described. For the moment, however, we will not consider models such as $F_{ij} = \eta \, \tau_{ij}^{VM}$.

The various general log-linear models we discussed above are presented in their multiplicative form. We note that by taking natural logarithms of all the terms, the equations can be transformed into linear equations. That is, the equations are linear in their logarithms (Ln; hence, log-linear), whence the name for this methodology. In Goodman's notation, Equation 1 has the log-linear form:

$$F_{ij} = \eta \, \tau_i^V \, \tau_j^M \, \tau_{ij}^{VM} \tag{1}$$

$$Ln(F_{ij}) = Ln(\eta \, \tau_i^V \, \tau_j^M \, \tau_{ij}^{VM}) = Ln(\eta) + Ln(\tau_i^V) + Ln(\tau_j^M) + Ln(\tau_{ij}^{VM})$$

or

$$G_{ij} = \theta + \lambda_i^V + \lambda_j^M + \lambda_{ij}^{VM} \tag{15}$$

where the λs (lambdas) are logs of the taus, θ (theta) is the log of eta, and G_{ij} is the log of F_{ij}. The nonsaturated models have similar log-linear expressions. The log-linear versions are more analogous to ordinary regression: The log of the expected cell frequency is an additive function of a constant plus terms for each variable and their interrelationships. Since the natural log of 1.00 is zero, the absence of a lambda effect in a model is equivalent to a value of zero for that parameter, just as in ordinary regression a variable with no impact has a slope of zero.

The multiplicative and additive logarithmic forms are mathematically equivalent. The conceptual advantage of the multiplicative version lies in its closeness to the odds and odds ratio basis underlying the motivation of the models. Since both versions have gained currency in social science, the reader should develop some familiarity with working in both systems of notation.

The statistical significance of the effect parameters in the saturated model can most easily be determined when in their log-linear form (i.e., the λs). The standard error of the lambdas can be estimated by the equation (Goodman, 1972b: 1048):

$$\hat{s}_\lambda = \sqrt{\frac{\sum_i \sum_j (1/f_{ij})}{C^2}}$$

where C is the number of cells in the contingency table. For large samples, if the expected value of lambda is zero (i.e., tau = 1.00), the standardized λ (i.e., $\lambda / \hat{s}_\lambda$) is approximately normally distributed with zero mean and unit variance. Hence, as in ordinary regression, a standardized lambda larger than ± 1.96 would be significant at the p = .05 level. Although such standardization strictly applies only to saturated models, $\hat{s}_\lambda$ provides an upper bound test statistic for tests of significance of the parameters of an unsaturated model. For Table 1, $\hat{s}_\lambda$ = .029. Taking logs of the three taus for the saturated model and dividing by this standard error gives large standardized values, showing that all three effects are highly significant.

B. Fitting Marginals

We now introduce a conventional notation to describe models without resorting to the cell frequency equations used in the previous section. First, we elaborate on the concept of a hierarchical structure. A hierarchy of models exists whenever a complex multivariate relationship present in the data necessitates inclusion of less complex interrelationships. For example, in the four-variable crosstabulation, if a hierarchical model is designated which includes the three-way interaction of vote, membership, and education (τ^{VME}), the equation for that model must also include all two-variable parameters (τ^{VM}, τ^{ME}, and τ^{VE}) as well as the single-variable effects (τ^{V}, τ^{M}, and τ^{E}) and of course the grand mean effect, η. In a hierarchical structure, models containing higher order relationships implicitly include all combinations of lower order effects which can be formed out of the components of the former. Log-linear methods encompass both hierarchical and nonhierarchical approaches, although the former type are generally preferred for reasons discussed later in this paper. In fact, some log-linear estimation methods do not allow the researcher to include higher order associations while omitting lower order terms which are nested within them.

The shorter notation for describing models uses letters which stand for the specific variables in the crosstabulation. It encloses letters of variables which are hypothesized by the model to be related within curly braces or parentheses. Each set of letters within braces indicates a highest order effect parameter included in the model (i.e., the taus which are not set equal to 1.00 by hypothesis in the multiplicative or equal to 0 in the additive version). By virtue of the hierarchical requirement, the set of letters within braces reveals all the lower order relationships which are necessarily present. To illustrate, the saturated model for the data in Table 1 was written in Equation 1:

$$F_{ij} = \eta \ \tau_i^V \ \tau_j^M \ \tau_{ij}^{VM} \qquad [1]$$

while in the standard notation, its designation is {VM}. By putting both V and M within the same pair of braces (the order of the letters is not important) we specify that the one-variable taus for vote {V} and membership {M} are also present, as is η. If the model in Equation 11 is hypothesized, the notation is simply {V} {M}. Since the letters for vote and membership do not appear within the same braces, we interpret this as a model in which V and M are hypothesized to be unrelated to each other, although the marginal odds for either may differ from 1.00.

To extend this notation to the four-way table crosstabulating race, education, membership, and vote turnout, the saturated model would be designated {REMV}. If the researcher hypothesizes that this four-way interaction is not necessary to fit the data but that all three-way interactions are required, the new model would be compactly written {REM} {REV}{RMV}{EMV}. In a greatly simplified model, such as {EV}{EM}

{R}, we can grasp quickly that no four- or three-way interactions are hypothesized, most of the two-way associations are absent and for the race variable only the marginal odds are hypothesized as necessary to fit the data.

Besides compactness of expression, the standard notation for log-linear models communicates another important feature of the analysis. The variables enclosed in braces designate subtables ("marginal" tables) formed from the full crosstabulation. In estimating expected cell frequencies for the full table under a given hypothesized model, the expected frequencies (F_{ij}'s) in the designated marginals must exactly equal the corresponding observed frequencies (f_{ij}'s) in the same set of subtables. Procedures used to estimate the expected frequencies (described in the next section) insure that the expected frequencies will always fit the observed frequencies for the specified marginals. Therefore, the standard notation is often called the *fitted marginals* notation.

This concept is implicit in the traditional chi-square test for independence in a two-way table such as the V-M crosstabulation of Table 1. In this test, one requirement of the expected cell frequencies is that they sum to the observed row and column marginal frequencies. In standard log-linear notation, the model for independence, {V}{M}, means that the single-variable marginal distributions for the vote and for membership "fitted" to the data by the model must exactly equal the row and column totals observed in the crosstabulation. If the model {V}{M} is fitted to the data in Table 1, the following expected frequencies are found:

| | | Membership (M) | | |
		One or More	None	Total
Vote Turnout	Voted	617.13	369.87	987
	Not Voted	303.87	182.13	486
		921	552	1473

Although the F_{ij}'s of this model differ from the f_{ij}'s, collapsing (adding) across rows and columns yields marginals equal to the observed data. Note also that the odds ratio of the expected frequencies is 1.00, in conformance with the model's hypothesis that $\tau^{VM} = 1.00$, meaning the two variables are unrelated.

The "marginals" of a two-way table are clearly the row or column totals, corresponding to the distribution of cases across the categories of any variable. In multiway crosstabulations, marginals can refer to two-variable, three-variable, or larger subtables formed upon collapsing the larger table according to the pattern hypothesized in the fitted marginal notation for a model. Even a saturated log-linear model has a fitted marginal table; it just happens to be equal to the observed table, hence the equivalence of fitted and observed cell frequencies for a saturated model.

We can illustrate some of these ideas with the complete four-way table of race, education, membership, and vote turnout, whose observed frequencies are shown in Table 3. Suppose we hypothesize that the vote is separately related to membership, jointly related to race and education (i.e., a three-variable interaction), and that race, education, and membership are also mutually related. In fitted marginal notation, this model is {VM}{VRE}{REM}. Using a procedure, to be explained shortly, for estimating the expected frequencies under this model, we find the frequencies shown in Table 4. We leave it for the reader to verify that if the appropriate entries of expected F_{ijkl}'s are summed to produce the three marginals fitted by the model the results will exactly equal the same marginal sums of the observed frequencies. Note also that lower order associations nested within the higher order marginals—such as {VR} {RE} and {EM}—will also agree in both observed and modelled data.

Generating expected frequencies. At this point we need to explain how to produce the expected frequencies for a hypothesized model. For some simple models, such as the two-variable models examined above, simple formulas exist which permit direct estimates for nonsaturated models to be written. But for larger tables and more complex models, some sort of algorithm is required to obtain the expected frequencies of the model. The two usual procedures are the *iterative proportional fitting algorithm* (Deming-Stephan algorithm) used by Fay and Goodman's ECTA program and the *Newton-Raphson algorithm* used in Bock's MULTIQUAL program. Although the Newton-Raphson procedure is more general, we shall continue most of our discussion with the simpler and more frequently used iterative proportional fitting algorithm.

The computer implementation of the iterative proportional algorithm is fairly complicated and will not be presented here (Davis, 1974: 227-231; Bishop et al., 1975: 57-122; Goodman, 1972b: 1080-1085; Fienberg, 1977: 33-36). The procedure uses the marginal tables fitted by the model to insure that the expected frequencies sum across the other variables to

TABLE 3
Crosstabulations of Race, Education, Membership and Vote Turnout

Race	Education	Membership	Vote Turnout	
			Voted	Not Voted
White	Less than High School	None	114	122
White	Less than High School	One or More	150	67
White	High School Graduate	None	88	72
White	High School Graduate	One or More	208	83
White	College	None	58	18
White	College	One or More	264	60
Black	Less than High School	None	23	31
Black	Less than High School	One or More	22	7
Black	High School Graduate	None	12	7
Black	High School Graduate	One or More	21	5
Black	College	None	3	4
Black	College	One or More	24	10

TABLE 4
Expected Cell Frequencies for Model $\{VM\}\{VER\}\{ERM\}$

Race	Education	Membership	Vote Turnout	
			Voted	Not Voted
White	Less than High School	None	116.76	119.23
White	Less than High School	One or More	147.24	69.77
White	High School Graduate	None	86.82	73.18
White	High School Graduate	One or More	209.18	81.82
White	College	None	52.82	23.18
White	College	One or More	269.18	54.82
Black	Less than High School	None	25.77	28.23
Black	Less than High School	One or More	19.23	9.77
Black	High School Graduate	None	12.27	6.73
Black	High School Graduate	One or More	20.73	5.27
Black	College	None	3.55	3.45
Black	College	One or More	23.45	10.55

equal the corresponding observed marginal totals. Expected odds and odds ratios among variables not constrained by the model's fitted marginals are all equal to 1.00.

The iterative proportional fitting process generates maximum likelihood estimates (MLE's) of the expected cell frequencies for a hierarchical model. Although an exposition of MLE techniques is beyond the scope of this book, these procedures produce consistent and efficient statistical estimates, two criteria highly desirable on theoretical grounds (see Bishop et al., 1975: 58). Preliminary estimates of the expected cell frequencies are successively adjusted to fit each of the marginal subtables specified in the model. (Typically all cell entries are initially estimated as 1. Since conversion to final estimates is very rapid, this seldom presents problems. Later we present analyses where different starting values are used.) Thus, in the model {VM}{VRE}{REM} the initial estimates are adjusted first to fit {VM}, then to fit {VRE}, and finally to equal the {REM} observed frequencies. With each new fit, however, the previous adjustment becomes somewhat distorted, so the process starts over again with the most recent cell estimates. Each cycling through the set results in some improvement, until an arbitrarily small difference between the current and previous estimate is reached, at which point the process concludes.

This MLE algorithm always converges to as small a discrepancy between successive estimates of the expected frequencies as desired. Although Davis (1974) gives the rules necessary to carry out the calculations with a pocket calculator, only the simplest problems can be calculated without a high-speed computer.

After the program produces the expected frequencies (F_{ij}'s) for a given model specification, these numbers are entered by the program into the appropriate formulas to produce the effect parameter estimates (taus or lambdas) for the variables and their interactions.

C. Analyzing Odds

Up to now we have dealt only with the general log-linear model. In that version, all variables are treated equally, as response variables whose relationships are to be determined by a multiplicative or additive function of the entire set of variables. The criterion to be modelled by the effect parameters is the expected cell frequency (F_{ij}). We now turn to the second major form of log-linear models, a special case of the general version called the logit model. Logit models are categorical variable analogs to ordinary linear regression models for continuous dependent variables. Indeed, Goodman (1972) called it a "modified regression approach." In this model, one variable is taken conceptually as dependent upon variation induced by the others. The criterion analyzed in this model is the odds of the expected cell frequencies for the dependent variable. More precisely, the model we discuss pertains to the log of the odds, called the *logit*. (Usually the logit is defined as 1/2 the log of the odds. However, Goodman has adopted the convention of analyzing the log odds, which we follow here; see Goodman, 1972: 35.)

To compare the logit model with the general log-linear model, we consider the three-variable case of voting, voluntary association membership, and race. Voting will be conceptualized as the dependent variable whose odds are a function of membership and race. Under the log-linear (saturated) model the expected cell frequency, F_{ijk}, is a function of various effect parameters. Thus,

$$F_{ijk} = \eta \, \tau_i^V \, \tau_j^M \, \tau_k^R \, \tau_{ij}^{VM} \, \tau_{ik}^{VR} \, \tau_{jk}^{MR} \, \tau_{ijk}^{VMR} \, .$$

Now, if we used these expected cell frequencies to form an expected odds on voting, we have the following:

$$\frac{F_{1jk}}{F_{2jk}} = \frac{\eta \tau_1^V \, \tau_j^M \, \tau_k^R \, \tau_{1j}^{VM} \, \tau_{1k}^{VR} \, \tau_{jk}^{MR} \, \tau_{1jk}^{VMR}}{\eta \tau_2^V \, \tau_j^M \, \tau_k^R \, \tau_{2j}^{VM} \, \tau_{2k}^{VR} \, \tau_{jk}^{MR} \, \tau_{2jk}^{VMR}} \, .$$

Once common terms on the top and bottom of this equation are cancelled, we arrive at the simplified expression:

$$\frac{F_{1jk}}{F_{2jk}} = \frac{\tau_1^V \, \tau_{1j}^{VM} \, \tau_{1k}^{VR} \, \tau_{1jk}^{VMR}}{\tau_2^V \, \tau_{2j}^{VM} \, \tau_{2k}^{VR} \, \tau_{2jk}^{VMR}} \, .$$

Given the further restrictions introduced earlier to achieve identifiability, this expression simplifies even more to:

$$\frac{F_{1jk}}{F_{2jk}} = (\tau^V)^2 \, (\tau_j^{VM})^2 \, (\tau_k^{VR})^2 \, (\tau_{jk}^{VMR})^2$$

and upon taking logs we get:

$$Ln \frac{F_{1jk}}{F_{2jk}} = 2Ln(\tau^V) + 2Ln(\tau_j^{VM}) + 2Ln(\tau_k^{VR}) + 2Ln(\tau_{jk}^{VMR})$$

or

$$Ln \frac{F_{1jk}}{F_{2jk}} = 2\lambda^V + 2\lambda_j^{VM} + 2\lambda_k^{VR} + 2\lambda_{jk}^{VMR}$$

where the λ's are natural logs of the taus. Reexpressing this in Goodman's (1972) notation we have:

$$\Phi_{jk}^V = \beta^V + \beta_j^{VM} + \beta_k^{VR} + \beta_{jk}^{VMR}.$$

We thus see that there is a direct relationship between the effect parameters of the log-linear model and the parameters of the logit model. Thus Φ_{jk}^V (phi) is the log of the (conditional) odds of voting, and the β's (betas) correspond to the lambdas, for example, $\beta^V = 2\lambda^V$, $\beta_j^{VM} = 2\lambda_j^{VM}$, and so on.

To illustrate the difference between the logit and the general log-linear model, we shall analyze the four-variable data. Suppose we hypothesize that the odds on turning out to vote depend on membership, race, education, and the interaction of race and education. Then the logit equation for this model, using Goodman's notation, is:

$$\Phi_{ijk}^V = \beta^V + \beta_i^{VM} + \beta_j^{VE} + \beta_k^{VR} + \beta_{jk}^{VER} \qquad [16]$$

where Φ^V is the log of the expected odds on the vote turnout. Consistent with the restrictions on the equivalent log-linear model, the β's for each factor influencing V sum to zero. For example, since education has three categories, $\beta_1^{VE} + \beta_2^{VE} + \beta_3^{VE} = 0$.

An important aspect of the logit model which is not evident from Equation 16 is that the three-way interaction among all independent variables {REM} is present as are all lesser included marginals {RE}, {RM}, {EM}, {R}, {E}, {M}. Terms for these factors do not appear in the logit equation for the expected odds on voting but these marginals must be fitted when estimating the expected frequencies on which the odds are based. The marginal table in which all independent variables interact must be included in any logit model even if the factor is not statistically significant (by criteria to be discussed in the next section). This inclusion is a major difference in the estimating procedure of the logit and the general log-linear models and the reasoning for it is as follows. Using the fitted marginals notation (explained above) for the four-variable case we can compare the following two models: {VMER} and {V}{MER}. The first of these is, of course, the saturated model in which all effects are present. The second model is restricted in a very special way. The following effects are presumed to be zero (absent): {VM}{VE}{VR}{VME} {VER}{VMR}{VMER}, that is, all relationships and interactions involving voting turnout. And these are the only effects assumed to be zero in the latter model. If we wish to test whether any of the effects involving V are necessary to model the data accurately, such tests are carried out by comparison with a baseline model, like {V}{MER}, which includes only (and all) relationships not involving the dependent variable. This log-linear procedure is analogous to regression analysis since the correlations among the independent variables are taken into account even though these relationships do not explicitly appear in the regression equation.

Estimation of parameters for Equation 16 begins, as in the general log-linear model, with fitting the marginals implied by the hypothesis to obtain the expected frequencies. The fitted marginals {MER}{ERV} {MV} produce the expected values in Table 4. Note the wide range of logits, from $-.09$ [= Ln (25.77/28.23)] for blacks without high schooling and no membership to 1.59 [= Ln (269.18/54.82)] for whites with college education and some memberships. To obtain the beta values we transform appropriate taus using the relationship (where Q stands for other variables affecting V):

$$\beta^{VQ} = 2 \; Ln\tau^{VQ}$$

since Goodman's definition of the logit is twice the value of the usual definition. Table 5 gives the relevant taus and their beta equivalents for the model in Equation 16.

A log-linear program, such as ECTA, can be used to estimate β's for the logit model in one of two ways. Estimates of the λ's may be obtained as suggested above (page 25) and these values doubled to obtain the equivalent β's. Alternatively, the odds of the dependent variable may be read in directly as observed values in which case the λ's of the additive version of the general log-linear model are then directly equivalent to the β's of the logit model (using Goodman's notation). Either way, the fit of the model to the data will be identical.

To show that these parameters exactly reproduce the expected odds, let us write the equation for blacks with high school graduation and some memberships. The expected odds that these respondents voted in 1976 are 20.73 to 5.27; the logit is 1.37. The equation for this logit is:

$$\Phi_{222}^{V} = \beta^{V} + \beta_{2}^{VM} + \beta_{2}^{VE} + \beta_{2}^{VR} + \beta_{22}^{VER}.$$

TABLE 5
τ and β Parameters for Model $\{VM\}\{VER\}\{ERM\}$

Term	τ	β
η	1.375	.636
τ_{11}^{VM}	0.825	−.385
τ_{11}^{VR}	1.037	.073
τ_{11}^{VE}	0.857	−.309
τ_{12}^{VE}	1.069	.133
τ_{13}^{VE}	1.091	.174
τ_{111}^{VER}	0.982	−.036
τ_{121}^{VER}	0.866	−.288
τ_{131}^{VER}	1.176	.324

Parameter values reported for level 1 of R (white) and level 1 of M (some memberships). Values for other levels can be obtained by taking reciprocals (for T) or changing sign (for β).

Plugging in the appropriate β values (note the change in signs when membership and race are at level 2):

$$\Phi_{222}^{V} = .636 + .385 + .133 - .073 + .288 = 1.37.$$

The parameters in the logit model can be interpreted similarly to the additive coefficients of ordinary regression. Positive values indicate that the independent variable or interaction raises the odds on the dependent measure, while negative betas show that the odds are decreased. Thus, having no membership substantially reduces turnout (−.385) while being white raises it slightly (.073). To evaluate a polytomous independent variable, all the betas must be considered. Being low in education depresses turnout (−.309) but increasing levels of schooling raises the odds on voting (.133 for high school graduation and .174 for college). Interaction effects can be substantively interpreted in more than one way. For example, the $\beta_{31}^{VER} = .324$ can be interpreted either as indicating that college education improves voter turnout more for whites than for blacks or that being white improves voter turnout more among college-educated than among less-educated respondents. By itself, this coefficient does not indicate that college-educated whites have a higher turnout than either college-educated blacks (although they do) or than less-educated whites (although that also is true). It indicates only that the log odds for cell 231 is greater than would be expected from the equivalent model which excludes this effect; that is,

$$\Phi_{231}^V = \beta^V + \beta_2^{VM} + \beta_3^{VE} + \beta_1^{VR}.$$

This is an important point about interpreting the effect parameters and it is worth expanding on a bit at this point. Consider the hypothetical table of data (Table 6) indicating the relationship between the presence or absence of A and the presence or absence of B. If we calculate a chi-square for Table 6 (8.56, df = 1), we would find a significant relationship between the variables such that those persons who are in category A also tend to be in category B. But, note that statement compares the observed frequency of 54 persons who are both A and B with an expected frequency (on the basis of the marginal distributions) for that cell of 38.72. In terms of simple raw frequencies, persons who are in category A are more likely to be in category non-B (as is everyone, A or non-A). A more complete description of the data would say something like: "Although most persons are in the category non-B, those persons who are A's are comparatively less likely to be in this category and more likely to be in the category B." In the context of log-linear models, therefore, we must be clear that the effect parameters indicate differences in *relative* frequencies and in *relative* odds and odds ratios. In the table above, being an A improves one's chances of being a B (though they continue to remain low).

TABLE 6
The Relationship Between the Presence or Absence of A and B

	A	Non-A	Total
B	54 (38.72)	187 (202.28)	241 (241)
Non-B	187 (202.28)	1072 (1056.72)	1259 (1259)
Total	241 (241)	1259 (1259)	1500 (1500)

3. TESTING FOR FIT

A. How To Evaluate Models Fitted to Data

We have now shown how to conceptualize log-linear models in either general or logit form and how to designate relationships among variables using both the equations and fitted-marginals notations. We also indicated other sources for discussions of how expected frequencies can be obtained, either with direct formulas or through iterative proportional fitting computer algorithms. We are now ready to discuss how to determine whether a hypothesized model fits the observed data reasonably well. For example, Equations 1 and 11 to 14 are five distinct models applying to the two-way crosstabulation in Table 1, yet only one of these models can represent the process by which the observed frequencies were generated. Our question is how to decide which model provides the best fit.

This question is answered by estimating the expected cell frequencies, F_{ij}'s, for each of the five models and comparing them to the observed frequencies, f_{ij}'s, using either the Pearson chi-square statistic (χ^2) or the likelihood-ratio statistic:

$$L^2 = 2\Sigma f_{ij} \ln (f_{ij}/F_{ij}). \qquad [17]$$

L^2 is preferable to χ^2 because (1) the expected frequencies are estimated by maximum likelihood methods and (2) L^2 can be partitioned uniquely for more powerful tests of conditional independence in multiway tables. L^2 follows the chi-square distribution with degrees of freedom (df) equal to the number of tau parameters set equal to 1.00 (no effect on expected cell frequencies). (See Davis, 1974, for a detailed discussion of determining degrees of freedom in multivariable log-linear models.) The larger the L^2 relative to the available df, the more the expected frequencies depart from the actual cell entries. Hence, we conclude for large L^2 that the hypothesized model does not fit the data well and should be rejected as an inadequate representation of the relationships among the variables.

Note that this testing strategy is the opposite of the one usually taught in conjunction with traditional chi-square tests of independence in two-way tables and thus might cause some confusion about the decision-making procedure. In the usual chi-square test of independence, we seek to *reject* the null hypothesis of no association between the variables; hence, we hope to find a large χ^2 value relative to df. But in trying to find the best-fitting log-linear or logit model to describe a crosstabulation, we hope to *accept* the hypothesized model; hence, we want to find a low L^2 value relative to df.

One further caution about statistical testing: An acceptable log-linear model is one whose expected cell frequencies do not significantly differ from the observed data. As a result, the analyst has a difficult choice to make with respect to the level of Type I error (alpha) she or he is willing to choose. Typically in trying to generalize sample results to a population, we set alpha very small—such as $p = .05$ or $.01$—not wishing to conclude that a relationship exists unless strong evidence is mustered that the null hypothesis is wrong.

But the strategy of finding the "best" fitting model impels greater interest in Type II error (beta), over which less control is possible. We want to identify the one model which contains all the true relationships, but if Type II error has a high probability we are likely to omit effects from the model which exist in the population. Type II errors can be reduced by either increasing the sample size (often infeasible, especially with secondary data sets) or by increasing the chances of Type I error. The second alternative poses the dilemma of potentially including relationships in the model which should not be included since they reflect only sampling variation. Probably the most frequent solution to this problem is the decision to accept a model as fitting the data if the probability of a Type I error lies between about .10 and .35. At higher probability levels, the model may involve "too good a fit," that is, include unnecessary parameters (Bishop et al., 1975: 324).

To illustrate the model-testing process, we will evaluate each of the five models for the two-way data in Table 1. The results are shown in Table 7. All except one of these models have L^2 values too large to be acceptable. Only the saturated model 1, which fits the data perfectly but uses all the degrees of freedom, tells the story. Notice that to evaluate a saturated model, we must compare its fit to that obtained by a non-saturated model omitting the full interaction term (i.e., compare model 1 to model 11). This intermodel comparison strategy is explored in the next section.

B. Comparisons of Different Models of the Same Data

Hypotheses can be understood as explicit comparisons between alternative models fitted to the same data. The five models for the vote-by-membership crosstabulation (Equations 1 and 11 to 14) can be compared

TABLE 7
Comparisons Among Models for Data in Table 1

Model	Fitted Marginals	Effect Parameters				Likelihood Ratio L^2	d.f.	p
		η	τ_1^V	τ_1^M	τ_{11}^{VM}			
1	$\{VM\}$	331.66	1.37	0.83	0.80	0.00	0	—
11	$\{V\}\{M\}$	335.25	1.43	0.77	1.00*	66.78	1	<.001
12	$\{V\}$	346.30	1.43	1.00*	1.00*	160.22	2	<.001
13	$\{M\}$	356.51	1.00*	1.29	1.00*	240.63	2	<.001
14	$\{\ \}$	368.25	1.00*	1.00*	1.00*	334.07	3	<.001

*Set to 1.00 by hypothesis.

two at a time to test several hypotheses about effects present in the data. These hypotheses are not independent of each other, however. Because there are only four independent parameters, yet 10 possible comparisons (hypotheses) among the five models, it is clear that the comparisons overlap. For example, the results of comparing Equation 11 with 12 (a test of τ_i^M) is obviously not independent of the results of comparing Equation 13 with 14 (also a test of τ_i^M, though in this case the effects of V are not controlled). While many hypotheses are possible, we will consider two fundamental questions which could be answered with the L^2 values in Table 7.

Independence hypothesis. The most usual and plausible question to ask of the data in Table 1 is whether the vote turnout and organizational membership are independent. The traditional chi-square test could show that the two are not independent, as the second line in Table 7 shows. But in a formal test of the independence hypothesis, we are in fact comparing the results of model 1 with model 11. The difference between these two models, as can be seen in contrasting Equations 1 and 11, is the presence of the τ_{ij}^{VM} in the former but not the latter. If the two models give different L^2's, it can only be because the tau parameter for the two-variable association reflects a significant covariation of these variables. Substantively, the odds ratio which compares the odds on voting turnout among nonmembers to the turnout odds among members must differ significantly from 1.00 (the "no effect" value of tau in the multiplicative version of the general log-linear model).

The test of the difference between the two models substracts the L^2 values and compares it to the difference in degrees of freedom. This difference in L^2 is also distributed approximately as a chi-square variable with df equal to the difference in df's between the two models. For the particular example, Table 7 shows $\Delta L^2 = (66.78 - 0.00) = 66.78$ and $\Delta df = (1 - 0) = 1$, highly significant at less than .001. Thus, we reject the null hypothesis and conclude that vote turnout and membership are significantly related in the population from which this sample was drawn. (Practically, we should deflate the L^2 value by one-third to take into account the non-random sampling design employed by the General Social Survey [see Stephan and McCarthy, 1958]. However, since our analyses are merely illustrative, we conveniently ignore this modification. The substantive conclusions would remain unchanged in this instance.)

Equal marginal distributions hypothesis. These two hypotheses can be easily handled within the log-linear framework, although their substantive value for this particular example is nil. Compare Equations 11 and 12. Their difference is the hypothesized absence of the τ^M parameter in the latter. The term's value is a function of the odds on not belonging to any voluntary association relative to belonging. To the degree that non-members are in the minority, the observed marginal odds will depart from 1:1, hence the τ^M term will be less than 1.00. Whether this departure is significant depends on the difference between the likelihood ratio test statistics for the two models differing only in the presence and absence of this parameter. Since $\Delta L^2 = 93.44$ for $\Delta df = 1$, we readily conclude that the marginals are not equally split on the membership variable. A similar decision for the equal-marginal distribution hypothesis on voting turnout can be calculated.

The two types of hypotheses tested above are simple hypotheses about the effects of single parameters. More complex hypotheses could be tested in which entire groups of parameters are compared simultaneously between two models. For example, by comparing model 14 to model 11, we can test both marginal inequalities at once. (What decision would we reach?) But the more frequent application of incremental testing is to determine whether specific parameters are required to provide acceptable fits of the model to the observed data.

C. More Complex Models: Polytomous Variables

We have already looked briefly at the four-way table of vote, membership, education, and race using equations with the voting logit as a function of the other three. A closer look at several additional features of this multiway analysis is warranted. Consider first the equation for a saturated general log-linear model:

$$F_{ijkl} = \eta \tau_i^V \, \tau_j^M \, \tau_k^E \, \tau_l^R \, \tau_{ij}^{VM} \, \tau_{ik}^{VE} \, \tau_{il}^{VR} \, \tau_{jk}^{ME} \, \tau_{jl}^{MR} \, \tau_{kl}^{ER}$$

$$\tau_{ijk}^{VME} \, \tau_{ijl}^{VMR} \, \tau_{ikl}^{VER} \, \tau_{jkl}^{MER} \, \tau_{ijkl}^{VMER} \quad [18]$$

Incidentally, this fearsome-looking equation underscores the advantage of the fitted-marginal notation; the same model can be represented compactly by {VMER}.

Note that, in contrast to the two-variable Equation 1, several parameters are present to represent possible interactions among three and four variables. Such interaction terms may be conceptualized as conditional relationships: The magnitude of the odds ratio between any pair is contingent upon the level of the third or fourth variables. For example, τ_{jkl}^{MER} can mean that the association between educational level and membership varies with respondents' race, or that racial differences in education vary with membership level, or that membership rates by race are contingent on education. Which interpretation a researcher chooses to emphasize in the substantive example depends on the theoretical questions motivating the research.

From a statistical viewpoint, an interaction effect is a function of a ratio of odds ratios. When the odds ratio between a pair of variables at the first level of a third variable differs from the odds ratio at another level of the third variable, then this "odds ratio ratio" will depart from 1.00. However, if the odds ratio of the two variables is constant across categories of a third variable, then the tau parameter for the interaction will equal 1.00. As with other effects, restrictions are placed on three-variable taus; for example:

$$\tau^{VMR} = \tau_{111}^{VMR} = \tau_{122}^{VMR} = \tau_{212}^{VMR} = \tau_{221}^{VMR}$$

$$= \frac{1}{\tau_{112}^{VMR}} = \frac{1}{\tau_{121}^{VMR}} = \frac{1}{\tau_{211}^{VMR}} = \frac{1}{\tau_{222}^{VMR}} \cdot$$

$$[19]$$

That is, when all three variables are dichotomies, only one independent value of the effect parameter will be calculated and either that value or its reciprocal will apply to all eight combinations of the three dichotomies.

A further complication in model 18 arises from the inclusion of a variable, education, which is a polytomous variable (a trichotomy). Recall that tau parameters for dichotomous variables were functions of one numerical value: either that value or its reciprocal. But a trichotomy has two degrees of freedom and hence two unique effects (or their reciprocals) must be calculated.

The three τ_k^E parameters might be estimated several different ways, depending upon which of the three categories was chosen as the "baseline" from which to measure the odds. For example, one odds could contrast respondents in the first category (less than high school) with those in category two (high school grad). A second odds would relate the first category to the third (college). Both odds are independent of each other. But the third odds, contrasting categories two and three, could be derived from the other two odds. The ratio of the first odds to the second odds yields the odds on being college educated relative to being less than high school educated. Thus, there are only two independent odds which can be estimated with three categories. More generally, given K categories, K-1 different parameters or their reciprocals need be calculated.

In deciding which odds to calculate for estimates of the taus in Equation 18, we take advantage of the fact noted in Chapter 2 Section A that tau parameters represent the ratio of the number of cases expected in one category of a variable to the geometric average of the number expected in all categories. Thus the three τ_k^E's can be computed as:

$$\tau_1^E = \left\{ \begin{matrix} 2 & 2 & 2 \\ \pi & \pi & \pi \\ i & j & 1 \end{matrix} \left(\frac{F_{ij11}}{(F_{ij11}F_{ij21}F_{ij31})^{1/3}} \right) \right\}^{1/8} \qquad [20]$$

$$\tau_2^E = \left\{ \begin{matrix} 2 & 2 & 2 \\ \pi & \pi & \pi \\ i & j & 1 \end{matrix} \left(\frac{F_{ij21}}{(F_{ij11}F_{ij21}F_{ij31})^{1/3}} \right) \right\}^{1/8} \qquad [21]$$

$$\tau_3^E = \left\{ \begin{matrix} 2 & 2 & 2 \\ \pi & \pi & \pi \\ i & j & 1 \end{matrix} \left(\frac{F_{ij31}}{(F_{ij11}F_{ij21}F_{ij31})^{1/3}} \right) \right\}^{1/8} \qquad [22]$$

The π (pi) notation indicates multiplication of terms. Note that each tau is the reciprocal of the product of the other two, insuring that the joint product equals 1.00:

$$\tau_1^E = \frac{1}{\tau_2^E \tau_3^E} \qquad \tau_2^E = \frac{1}{\tau_1^E \tau_3^E} \qquad \tau_3^E = \frac{1}{\tau_1^E \tau_2^E} . \qquad [23]$$

Just as with the saturated model 1 for the two-way table, the saturated model 18 for the four-way table can give rise to simpler nonsaturated models by setting some of the tau parameters a priori equal to 1.00 (no effect). Even with just four variables and hierarchical models, a very large number of models can be evaluated. Table 8 presents summaries for some of these models, using the fitted-marginal notation. Making the substantive assumption that voting turnout, V, is the variable whose pattern we are interested in explaining as a function of the other three variables, each model fits the {MER} marginal table among these three. This is the procedure for logits that we outlined earlier in Chapter 2. The other fitted marginals, then, all involve V with one or more of the independent variables. In the next section we will discuss hypothesis testing to identify the best-fitting model of these data, but first we take up the matter of determining degrees of freedom in multivariable cross-tabulations.

To compute the degrees of freedom associated with a model, the number of categories of each variable must be known. In a four-way table with categories I, J, K, and L, respectively, the total degrees of freedom available are the total number of cells in the table less one or $(I)(J)(K)(L) - 1$. In the example $(M)(E)(R)(V) - 1 = (2)(3)(2)(2) - 1 = 23$ degrees of freedom available. A saturated model, of course, always has no available df since all conceivable parameters are free to vary in fitting the data precisely. As the number of parameters to be estimated from the data are reduced (by setting the corresponding taus equal to 1.00, hence the betas equal to 0) df's for testing the model are increased by the equivalent number.

Therefore, to determine df for any given model, we need only consider the variables included in each effect required for the model, count the number of categories in each, subtract one from each number, and multiply the set. For example, take model 28, fitting marginal tables {MER} {MV} {EV}. For the first subtable, membership and race both have two categories, education has three, so the number used is $(2-1)(2-1)(3-1) = 2$ df to fit this subtable. Since vote is a dichotomy, {MV} uses up $(2-1)(2-1) = 1$ df, while {EV} requires $(3-1)(2-1) = 2$ df. But remember that within higher

TABLE 8
Some Models for Data in Table 3

Model	Fitted Marginals	L^2	d.f.	p
24	{MER} {V}	104.23	11	.00
25	{MER} {MV}	37.44	10	.00
26	{MER} {EV}	51.92	9	.00
27	{MER} {RV}	102.21	10	.00
28	{MER} {MV} {EV}	10.96	8	.20
29	{MER} {MV} {RV}	36.74	9	.00
30	{MER} {EV} {RV}	51.11	8	.00
31	{MER} {MV} {EV} {RV}	10.66	7	.15
32	{MER} {MEV} {RV}	7.83	5	.17
33	{MER} {MRV} {EV}	10.05	6	.12
34	{MER} {ERV} {MV}	4.76	5	.45
35	{MER} {MEV} {ERV}	2.07	3	>.50

order relationships are nested the lower order relationships, in this case {ME}, {MR}, {ER}, {M}, {V}, {E}, and {R}, which consume 2, 1, 2, 1, 1, 2 and 1 additional df, respectively. Hence, 15 df's are used up in fitting this model. Since the total available is 23, the remaining df's for testing the model are 8. As a check, we can also calculate the df's for the marginal tables *not* fitted by the model. {RF} has 1 df, {MEV} has 2, {MRV} has 1, {ERV} has 2, and {MERV} has 2 which add up to the 8 degrees of freedom for testing the model. As expected, the two sets of df sum to 23 for the four-variable example.

D. More Complex Hypotheses

Many hypotheses about the effects of membership, education, and race on voting turnout might be examined using models such as those presented in Table 8. In substantive research, a data analyst's choice of models to investigate will typically be guided by theory and previous empirical findings. In the absence of explicit a priori hypotheses about the relationships among variables, one can still design a strategy model testing to locate the best fit to the observed data. Two general approaches seem most prevalent. One approach starts with the saturated model and begins successively deleting the higher order interaction terms until the fit of the model to the data becomes unacceptable by whatever probability standards the analyst has adopted. The second approach starts with the simplest model, such as one which fits only the one-variable marginal tables, and successively adds increasingly complex interaction terms until an acceptable fit is obtained which cannot be significantly improved by adding further terms. Ideally, both approaches converge upon the same hypothesized model as the best explanation of the observed relationships among variables. Our personal preference lies with the second approach, since it treats more parsimonious models as the starting point. Adding more complex relationships to simpler ones clearly reveals the hierarchical structure of the estimation methods we used for log-linear models.

Since we have already designated voting turnout as the dependent variable in the four-variable cross tabulation, a useful beginning model is one in which none of the independent variables has a significant relationship with the dependent measure. If this model provides an acceptable fit, no additional tests will be required. The model for testing this hypothesis has the general form of two fitted marginal tables:

{ all independent variables}{the dependent variable}

or, in the specific example, {MER}{V}.

The fit of this model is tested against the alternative in which the dependent variable is allowed to interact with all the independent variables. This alternative, of course, is the saturated model, or {MERV} in the example. If the difference in L^2 relative to the difference in df is significant, we conclude that one or more independent variables (or their interactions) significantly affects the dependent variable and must be included in the final model we select.

For the four-variable table, the relevant comparison is between model 24 in Table 8 and the saturated model (not shown, since it has no df and $L^2 = 0.0$). Since the difference between these two models is $\Delta L^2 = 104.23$ for only $\Delta df = 11$, we must reject model 24 and conclude that voting is indeed related to one or more independent variables.

The next set of models to be examined each add a single bivariate relationship involving voting turnout. Models 25, 26, and 27 are compared to model 24 to decide whether membership, education, and race, respectively, have significant effects on turnout. As before, the statistical criterion is whether the decrease in L^2 relative to the loss of degrees of freedom in estimating the additional parameters is significant (at $\alpha = .05$ in this case). Even if none of these models fits the four-variable table at an acceptable level, we can still determine whether specific two-variable effects must be included in subsequent models.

Both {MV} and {EV} substantially reduce the L^2 relative to their cost in degrees of freedom to fit these additional effects, although neither model 25 nor 26 yields an acceptable overall fit to the data. We conclude that turnout is significantly related to membership and to education in the four-way crosstabulation. However, the addition of {RV} to model 24 reduces L^2 by 2.02 for one df, not a significant improvement in fit. We conclude that voting turnout is unrelated to race.

The search for the best-fitting model continues with models 28, 29, and 30, each of which includes two of the three possible bivariate relationships involving the turnout variable. The amount of improvement in fit relative to df for these models is determined by comparisons to the preceding three models which contained only one bivariate marginal table.

As we should expect, neither model 29 nor model 30, both of which include the {RV} marginal table, significantly improves the fits obtained with models 25 and 26, respectively. Clearly, we will not find a significant impact of race on turnout. However, model 28 when compared to both models 25 and 26 shows a substantial drop in L^2 relative to df. Thus, even with one bivariate relationship held constant, the other bivariate effect is signficant. More important, model 28 gives an excellent overall fit to the full four-way table. Substantively, this model indicates that membership and education each affect turnout, net of the effects of each other. Our only remaining question is whether additional, higher order interaction terms must be included as well. Note that model 31, when compared to model 28, once again demonstrates that race is unrelated to turnout.

Given three independent variables, three trivariate interaction terms can be formed that involve voting turnout. Models 32, 33, and 34 each contain one of these interaction terms plus the two-variable marginal not subsumed within the interaction (to insure the hierarchical structure is preserved). The appropriate tests are conducted by comparing the amount of improvement in fit of each model relative to model 31. Although all three models provide acceptable fits to the data, neither the {MEV} nor the {MRV} interaction significantly improves the fit over the more parsimonious model 31 (nor are they superior to the even simpler model 28, for that matter). Model 34, however, which tests the {ERV} interaction, is more problematic. Compared to model 31, $\Delta L^2 = 5.90$ for $\Delta df = 2$. This difference is significant at the .06 probability level.

We may well wish to conclude that this interaction of education and race on turnout is essential to represent the relationships generating the data. But if we adhere strictly to statistical critieria and try to avoid Type I error, we will reject model 34 as not significantly better than either model 31 or model 28 and hence accept the hypothesis of no interaction effects. We seem to have encountered a gray area in which our conclusions may be influenced as much by the substantive aims which motivate the research as by strict statistical reasoning. Our own preference, in the absence of a confirmatory analysis with another sample and in the absence of any compelling theoretical argument for expecting that particular three-variable interaction, would be to choose the more parsimonious model 28, {MER}{MV}{EV}. That model gives a satisfactory fit to the full crosstabulation without resort to a complex three-variable interaction. It also omits the race-turnout effect which is known to be trivial, but which would have to be included in model 34 because it is subsumed in hierarchical relation to the {ERV} term. Perhaps a replication of this analysis on another data set from the General Social Survey would help resolve the question.

E. An Analog to Multiple R^2 for Large Samples

In our experience, using the L^2 tests of model significance works reasonably well as a guide to locating important effects in crosstabulations when the sample size is no greater than that for most national surveys (about 1500 cases). However, at times analysts will be interested in studying much larger data sets, such as census reports on the entire national population. The problem in judging best-fitting models is that L^2 is proportional to N. Hence, with potential samples in the hundreds of thousands or millions, virtually the only model which will be found to fit the data is the saturated model, even when some of the higher order interactions are very small.

To overcome this problem for large samples, analysts may approach model selection with an analog to the coefficient of determination (R^2) for multiple regression. A "baseline" model is selected whose L^2 will serve as a standard against which to judge the improvement in fit obtained by trying more complex alternative models. The baseline L^2 indicates the amount of variability in the data not due to factors already included in the model. When the proportion of the baseline L^2 accounted for by the alternative model is high (say, 90% or more), the alternative may be judged to provide a satisfactory fit to the data even though strict statistical tests

TABLE 9
Crosstabulation of Occupation, Sex, and Race, 1970 (thousands)

Occupation	White Men	White Women	Black Men	Black Women
Professional and Managerial	13,195	5,268	425	379
Clerical and Sales	5,865	11,587	436	712
Crafts	8,985	297	606	25
Operatives, Laborers, and Service Workers	13,343	8,739	2,623	2,187
Farmers and Farm Laborers	2,267	378	191	18

SOURCE: Current Population Reports Series P-23 No. 37, 1971. "Social and Economic Characteristics of the Population in Metropolitan and Nonmetropolitan Areas." Table 14, pp. 60-62.

indicate significant departure from expected frequencies under the alternative model. The R^2 analog is:

$$\frac{(L^2 \text{ baseline model}) - (L^2 \text{ alternative model})}{(L^2 \text{ baseline model})} \quad [24]$$

To illustrate the usefulness of this technique, we analyze data from a census report on the occupational distribution (J) of sex (S) and race (R) groups in 1970, as shown in Table 9 where the cell frequencies are thousands of persons. In choosing a baseline model our preference is to fit a model consisting of only one-way variable distributions, in this case $\{J\}\{S\}\{R\}$. The baseline $L^2 = 30,905$ for 13 df. Several two-variable alternative models reduce the L^2: $\{JR\}\{SR\}$ has and $L^2 = 15,431$; $\{JS\}\{SR\}$ has an $L^2 = 9,562$; and $\{JS\}\{JR\}$ has an $L^2 = 3,706$. These three models account for 50%, 69%, and 88%, respectively, of the baseline model variation. While substantial, no percentage is so large as to suggest that any of the three models accounts for the complete pattern of observed frequencies. However, when the full set of two-way marginals is fitted, $\{JS\}\{JR\}\{SR\}$, its $L^2 = 1,846$ (for df = 4), which captures 94% of the variation in the baseline model. Substantively, the model shows that occupations are differently distributed by sex and by race, but that sex differences are similar within race and race differences are similar within sex. $\{SR\}$ means that the sex ratio differs between the races. The proportion of variation explained is large enough to conclude that this model provides an acceptable fit to the data and that the interaction implied by the saturated model accounts for only 6% of the baseline model variation and that is small enough to ignore (though it is statistically significant).

4. APPLICATIONS TO SUBSTANTIVE PROBLEMS

The potential uses of log-linear models are virtually limitless. Any cross-tabulation can be analyzed using the basic techniques outlined in the preceding sections. In this section we touch upon a half-dozen applications which have fairly general appeal. Although each topic could be presented in greater detail than the present format permits, we hope our brief discussions convey the wide range of possibilities which readers may wish to pursue on their own.

A. Causal Models for Log-Linear Models

In describing how log-linear techniques may be adapted to test models of causal relationships among categoric variables, we shall assume the reader's familiarity with recursive causal models (those that include no "loops" or reciprocal effects between variables) in both their equation and path-diagram conventions. Basic expositions are available in Duncan (1966, 1975a) and Asher (1976). Goodman's (1973a, 1973b, 1979) efforts to draw a parallel between path analysis and a log-linear causal modelling have met with some success. The analogy breaks down however in (1) the inability of the log-linear version to assign single values to causal paths when polytomous variables are involved and (2) the calculation of the magnitude of effects along indirect paths between variables. Still, the causal analogy is sufficiently appealing to allow a tempered use of the method whenever a well-reasoned hypothesis can take advantage of uni-directional causal sequences among the variables.

The key to a causal model of relationships among variables is a diagram of recursive effects. In a causal diagram such as Figure 1, variables posited as causal antecedents of others are placed to the left of consequent variables. Single-headed arrows point from cause to effect. Variables among which no causal ordering can be posited are joined by curved two-headed arrows and must appear only on the left side of the diagram. Our causal

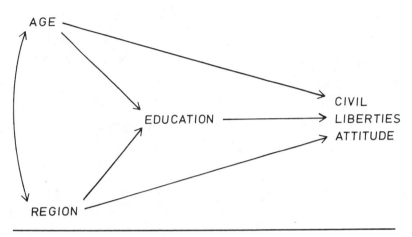

Figure 1: Causal Model Diagram

model was motivated by several assumptions: that respondents' ages (indexing their generation) and regional location were historical determinants of the amount of formal schooling received; that education, by exposing people to democratic values and norms of political tolerance, induces support for civil liberties; and, that both generational factors and regional culture have independent influences on civil liberties beliefs apart from education. We made no a priori assumptions about possible interaction effects of the three antecedent causes of civil liberties preferences, but our analysis will be open to testing for their presence.

The causal model was tested on data from the 1977 General Social Survey. For purposes of this illustration all four measures were dichotomized (though see Bishop et al., 1975, for a discussion of potential problems in dealing with such collapsed tables). Age was split at age 39 and under. Region was split between the South (including border states) and the rest of the United States. Education was divided between those with high school or less and those with at least some college. Finally, civil liberties attitude was operationalized as agreement or disagreement with one of the items used in Stouffer's (1955) classic study of tolerance: "Should an admitted Communist be allowed to deliver a speech in your community?"

The causal analysis of the data in Table 10 differs from the usual logit model (which is more akin to regression analysis with a single dependent

TABLE 10
Crosstabulation of Age, Region, Education, and Civil Liberties

Age	Region	Education	Communist Speaker	
			Allow	Not Allow
Young	South	No College	72	71
Young	South	College	55	22
Young	Non-South	No College	161	92
Young	Non-South	College	157	25
Old	South	No College	65	162
Old	South	College	23	23
Old	Non-South	No College	197	214
Old	Non-South	College	107	32

NOTE: Age dichotomized at 39 years and under, 40 years and older. Education dichotomized at 12 years or less, 13 years or more. South is all states in Census South and Border States.

variable and several independent variables). Causal modelling must take into account the temporal ordering among the four variables, fitting a succession of models to various "collapsed" tables constructed from the full table in a specific manner. We proceed in a series of independent steps, the results of each of which can be put together at the end.

Starting at the left in the diagram, we first form the two-way table of age by region and fit a series of log-linear models to determine whether these two "predetermined" measures are related to each other. Since {A}{R} has L^2 = .03 for df = 1, we conclude that the two variables are independent and should not be connected in the diagram by a double-headed curved arrow. The odds on being young are roughly the same both in the South and outside the South.

The next step in finding the best-fitting causal explanation is to analyze the three-way subtable formed from the two predetermined variables and the first dependent variable in the sequence, education. Even though the age and region variables were found in the previous step to be independent, the logit model we are estimating requires that the marginal table for all causal antecedents be automatically fitted. Hence, analyses of the causal structure of the age-region-education subtable must include the {AR} marginal table. The only models to be tested are those involving the relationship of education with the two antecedents, as shown in Table 11. Both the age-education and region-education associations are significant and required to fit the data, but the three-way interaction is not essential.

TABLE 11

Models Fitted to Three-Way Crosstabulation of Age, Region,
and Education Formed by Collapsing Data in Table 10

Fitted Marginals	L^2	d.f.	p
{AR}{E}	61.00	3	.00
{AR}{RE}	51.71	2	.00
{AR}{AE}	10.58	2	.01
{AR}{RE}{AE}	0.76	1	.38

The model for this step is thus {AR}{RE}{AE} and has $L^2 = .76$ with df = 1.

Finally, the third step in the analysis sequence treats the civil liberties attitude as the dependent measure, fitting the three-way marginal {ARE} in the process of identifying the best logit model to explain the observed frequencies in the full four-way table. Table 12 shows the results from the series of possible models. Once again we see that all three two-variable effects on the civil liberties item are necessary but that adding any three-way interactions would not significantly improve the already excellent fit provided by {ARE}{RS}{AS}{ES}. This model has $L^2 = 2.92$ with df = 4.

At this point we cumulate the results of the above analyses. The recursive causal model which best represents the data in Table 10 is the sum of the models for the successive two-, three-, and four-way crosstabulations. This model fits the marginal tables {A}{R}{AR}{RE}{AE}{RS} {AS}{ES} and has $L^2 = (.03 + .76 + 2.92) = 3.71$ with df = (1 + 1 + 4) = 6. Parameter estimates for the causal effects are the beta coefficients from the logit model described earlier. These are shown in Figure 2 with the final causal diagram. Since the entire system is composed of dichotomous variables, the single betas for each partial relationship may be interpreted as effects of the independent variables on the odds (logged) of the dependent variables. Thus we can see that older persons tend to have lower education, while those living outside the South have a greater chance of some college experience. The odds on holding a tolerant civil liberties attitude are raised by college education and living outside the South but are lower among older persons. Unlike path coefficients for systems of quantitative variables, we cannot legitimately multiply the paths linking age or region to attitude via education to estimate the size of the indirect causal effects. But by noting the signs of these compound paths, we can

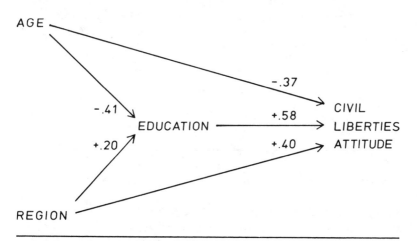

Figure 2: Final Causal Model

TABLE 12
Models Fitted to Four-Way Crosstabulation of Age, Region, Education, and Civil Liberties Attitude in Table 10

Fitted Marginals	L^2	d.f.	p
{ARE} {S}	200.48	7	.00
{ARE} {RS}	149.57	6	.00
{ARE} {AS}	138.48	6	.00
{ARE} {ES}	87.75	6	.00
{ARE} {RS} {AS}	84.72	5	.00
{ARE} {RS} {ES}	44.74	5	.00
{ARE} {AS} {ES}	48.69	5	.00
{ARE} {RS} {AS} {ES}	2.92	4	>.50

see that the indirect effects of the two predetermined variables operate in the same direction as do the direct causal paths. We can also compare the magnitudes of the betas for direct effects (since both are in the standard form of odds ratios) to judge the relative importance of the causes. Education has somewhat greater direct impact on civil liberties attitude than do either of the other two variables.

Our causal exploration of these variables uncovered no interaction terms which were significant. Had such marginal tables been required to fit the data, their representation in the causal diagram could have taken one of two forms: (1) the letter symbols of the two (or more) inter-acting causes could be placed inside a circle, with an arrow drawn from the circle to the dependent variable involved in the interaction, or (2) inter-action can be depicted by drawing an arrow from one of the independent variables to the midpoint of the arrow connecting the other independent variable to the dependent symbol. If many interactions are present, use of the first convention should result in a less cluttered-looking diagram. While we emphasized causal analysis involving dichotomous variables, nothing in theory prevents extension to polytomous variables. However, with three or more categories, three or more beta coefficients are produced and their representation in diagrams can become cumbersome. At this point the analogy to path analysis with standardized regression coefficients begins to break down and perhaps this accounts for the restriction to dichotomous variable models in practice.

B. Analyzing Change Over Time

As the social sciences mature, the availability of time series data on individuals increases. The capacity to study individual change in social behavior with log-linear methods has not been fully explored, but several basic techniques have been established. In this section we will touch upon applications to two forms of survey data: (1) the comparative cross-section study in which two or more survey replications are conducted but not necessarily with the same set of respondents and (2) the panel survey, in which the same individuals are reinterviewed on the same items at two or more points in time. Much work on methods of analysis for quantitative measures is generalizable to the discrete variable case.

Comparative cross-sections. When the same set of items are measured by surveys conducted at two points in time, a fundamental question is, "Do these variables covary to the same extent across time?" With quanti-tative measures we might attempt to answer this question by looking at the size of the correlations, regressions, or variance-covariance matrices, perhaps using methods developed by Jöreskog (1970). When categoric measures are involved, the effort to answer the question takes the form of comparing the odds or odds ratios from the different surveys and fitting a single log-linear model to frequencies from all data sets. The unique feature from a comparative cross-sections analysis is the explicit intro-duction of a variable for time (T). To the extent that T is associated with one of the substantive variables, the marginal distribution of that variable has changed over time. To the degree that T interacts with two or more substantive variables, the magnitude of the association between these variables has changed significantly.

Our illustration of the comparative cross section analysis uses General Social Survey data on the relationship between party identification and the partisan vote for presidential candidates in 1972 and 1976. While the vote is sometimes taken as a consequence of subjective party identification, in this problem we shall view them both as consequent variables. Our main interest is in the magnitude of covariation between the pair at the two time points. In Table 13 the crosstabulation of party (P), presidential vote (V), and time (T) is shown. The distributions reflect the well-known defection of Democrats in 1972 to Nixon, with 1976 restoring the more typical pattern of partisans voting overwhelmingly for their party's candidate and Independents roughly evenly split.

The question of whether this party-vote association differs between elections can be tested by fitting the nonsaturated model, which leaves out the three-variable interaction, and comparing the results to the saturated model, which fits the data perfectly. The model {TP}{TV}{PV} has $L^2 = 1.88$ with df = 2. Hence, the best-fitting log-linear model need not include the interaction effect, TPV, thus indicating no significant change in the PV relationship over time contrary to superficial appearances in Table 13. Expected frequencies for the {TP}{TV}{PV} model are given in Table 13. The two bivariate relationships, TP and TV, have substantive interpretations. They indicate that it is the marginal distributions of the vote choice and of party identification (within categories of the other variables) which change between times of measurement.

Two-wave panels. When respondents are reinterviewed with the same items at a later point in time, the survey is a two-wave panel. Our discussion in this section will be confined to the analysis of change in one variable between the two observation periods, although we realize some of the most interesting hypotheses concern the joint changes in two variables. On this latter topic, the reader is advised to consult articles by Goodman (1973, 1979) and Duncan (1980). Our analysis focuses on so-called "square tables" (in which the number of categories in the row and column variables is the same, i.e., a K X K table), which is typical not only of panel data but also such substantive problems as occupational mobility and comparisons of spouses' responses.

TABLE 13
Crosstabulation of Party Identification,
Presidential Vote Choice, and Time

| Time | Party Identification | Observed (Expected) Presidential Vote Choice | |
		Democrat	Republican
1972	Democrat	290 (295.27)	136 (130.73)
1972	Independent	98 (92.15)	198 (203.85)
1972	Republican	13 (13.57)	250 (249.43)
1976	Democrat	380 (374.73)	67 (72.27)
1976	Independent	123 (128.85)	130 (124.15)
1976	Republican	29 (28.43)	227 (227.57)

When first- and second-time measures of the same variable are cross-tabulated in a square K X K table, one obvious statistical test to perform is the test for independence. Yet this test is really uninformative since we typically expect most individuals to remain in their initial states (categories), particularly if the time between observations is fairly short. Thus, to learn that there is an association between the measures at two points in time does not tell us much about the nature of the changes which do occur. There are three models which can be fitted to the data and which yield greater insights into the pattern of changes over time. It is these which we shall discuss. These models can be used to test the hypotheses of marginal homogeneity, symmetry, and quasi-symmetry, or H_{MH}, H_S, and H_{QS} for short. Below we give explicit meanings to these hypotheses and show how L^2 values to test these models can be derived directly or indirectly from various log-linear specifications.

Marginal homogeneity is easiest to state. A square table has homogeneous marginals if the corresponding row and column marginal distributions are equal; that is, if $f_i. = f_{.j}$. Unfortunately, we cannot write a simple log-linear model for the expected values of the internal cells of the table for this model. Instead we must approach marginal homogeneity in a round-about way, taking advantage of the fact that there is a known relationship among the three hypotheses: H_{MH}, H_S, and H_{QS}. Before looking at this relationship, let us first present the other hypotheses of symmetry and quasi-symmetry.

Symmetry is said to exist when the pattern of changes between categories is exactly balanced. In terms of a square table, if $f_{ij} = f_{ji}$ for $i \neq j$ (for all off-diagonal cells), then a table has a symmetrical pattern. "Folding" the table along the diagonal would show identical frequencies in the corresponding cells. For example, in mobility studies in which father's occupation is crosstabulated with son's occupation, a symmetric table would indicate not only equal amounts of upward and downward mobility, but equal patterns of such as well. Note that symmetrical tables must display marginal homogeneity since rows and columns having identical entries must have identical sums. But marginal homogeneity does not imply symmetry since identical sums can be reached in numerous different ways.

Maximum likelihood estimates of the expected cell frequencies, F_{ij}, under the symmetry hypothesis for a square table are easily obtained by averaging the two appropriate observed frequencies:

$$F_{ij} = F_{ji} = (f_{ij} + f_{ji})/2 \qquad i \neq j. \qquad [25]$$

Since the diagonal cells are not involved in the hypothesis, the degrees of freedom are equal to half the number of off-diagonal cells (cell entries above the diagonal are not independent of those below the diagonal, and the diagonal cells are ignored): $df = k(k-1)/2$. The likelihood ratio chi-square test statistic takes the form

$$L^2 = 2 \sum_{i \neq j} f_{ij} \, Ln(f_{ij}/F_{ij}) \qquad [26]$$

which expresses the summation only for the off-diagonal cells.

An alternative (but identical) representation of the symmetry hypothesis through a log-linear model proceeds as follows. First, remove the diagonal cells from consideration. Split the remaining cells into two groups, an upper triangular matrix and a lower triangular matrix. "Flip" the upper triangular matrix over on its side so that it, too, becomes a lower triangular matrix which conforms to the corresponding row and column entries of the original lower triangular matrix. Putting these two together we thus obtain a three-dimensional array from the original two-way crosstabulation. For this let I represent the first (row) measure, J the second (column) measure, and M the two parts of the partition. Next, enter the three-way table into a log-linear analysis in which the missing entries in the upper right of each partition are represented as "structural zeros." That is, the models to be fitted will place zeros in these cells for expected values. (In terms of actually programming an algorithm such as ECTA, structural zeros are designated by a table of "starting values" in which 0 entries force the iterations continually to keep zeros present in those cells.)

Finally, to generate the expected cell frequencies which exhibit symmetry, the marginals fitted to this three-way data are {IJ}. Note the absence of any term involving M, the third variable created by splitting the original K × K table into two triangular parts. As before, the L^2 value obtained from comparing observed and expected frequencies should be evaluated against $K(K-1)/2$ df.

To illustrate the test for symmetry we examine data from the 1956-1960 Survey Research Center's panel study of the U.S. electorate. Specifically, we examine the 202 Catholic voters who reported a party identification for both elections. Previous analysis of these data showed a noticeable shift among Catholic voters away from the Republican and toward the Democratic party, presumably as a result of John Kennedy's candidacy (Knoke, 1976). The top panel of Table 14 indeed shows this change in the two marginals with both Independent and Republican categories declining between 1956 and 1960. When the symmetry model is fitted to the six internal off-diagonal cells, the expected frequencies are those shown in the lower panel of Table 14. For this hypothesis, $L^2 = 20.99$, with df = 3, which means we must reject the hypothesis that shifts in each direction tended to cancel each other.

Pursuing this example a bit, we first test whether the changes lie predominantly in one direction (toward Democratic or toward Republican) using the McNemar-like (see McNemar, 1962: 52ff.) test statistic

$$X^2 = (b - c)^2 / (b + c) \qquad [27]$$

where b is the sum of the observed frequencies on one side of the diagonal and c is the sum on the other side. Since $X^2 = 15.7$ for df = 1, we conclude that there is a significant tendency for net change to occur predominantly in one direction. Inspection of the table shows that to be in a Democratic direction.

The question then arises as to whether a modified form of symmetry holds in the table. That is, aside from the fact that there are fewer cases above than below the diagonal in Table 14, is the pattern of cases above and below the diagonal the same. The patterns are said to be the same if the odds ratios among the cells above the diagonals are identical with the odds ratios below the diagonal, even though absolute frequencies are not identical. This modified symmetry hypothesis fits the marginals {IJ}{M} to the three-way data involving the structural zeros, thereby preserving the total frequencies in each triangular part (which was not the case in true symmetry) but allowing the marginal distributions to vary freely. Table 15 presents both the observed frequencies and those expected

TABLE 14
Party Identification of Catholics in 1956-1960 SRC Panel

1956 Party Identification	1960 Party Identification			
	Democrat	Independent	Republican	Total
	A. Observed Data			
Democrat	100	4	1	105
Independent	19	30	6	55
Republican	11	9	22	42
Total	130	43	29	202
	B. Symmetry Model			
Democrat	100	11.5	6	117.5
Independent	11.5	30	7.5	49
Republican	6	7.5	22	35.5
Total	117.5	49	35.5	202

SOURCE: Knoke, 1976.

under the modified symmetry hypothesis for the three-dimension display. L^2 for this model is 4.36 with df = 2, so including the extra parameter to fit M (i.e., allowing change to occur predominantly in one direction) significantly improved the fit, reducing the L^2 by 16.63. This model supports the hypothesis that although the magnitude of the shift to each party is not the same, the pattern of the shifts is the same. That is, although the direction of change is unequal, there is symmetry conditional on that change.

Quasi-symmetry in a square table means that the condition of symmetry in the table is approached as closely as possible within the constraints of nonhomogeneity in the marginal distributions. While substantive applications of the test for symmetry are readily apparent, such is not the case for tests of quasi-symmetry. Indeed, its main use is to allow, indirectly as suggested above, a test for marginal homogeneity. The test becomes possible because the only difference between the model for symmetry and the model for quasi-symmetry is that the former includes an assumption of marginal homogeneity while the latter does not. The difference between the "fits" of each of these models with the data is a function entirely of the assumption of marginal homogeneity. Hence, the difference between the tests for quasi-symmetry and symmetry is a test for marginal homogeneity. We have already seen how to test for symmetry. We turn now to the test for quasi-symmetry.

TABLE 15
Three-Dimensional Display of Data in Table 14

| 1956 Party Identification | Shift Toward Democrat (Below Diagonal) | | | Shift Toward Republican (Above Diagonal) | | |
| | 1960 Party | | | 1960 Party | | |
	Dem.	Ind.	Total	Rep.	Ind.	Total
	A. Observed Frequencies					
Independent	19	—	19	6	—	6
Republican/Democrat	11	9	20	1	4	5
Total	30	9	39	7	4	11
	B. Expected Frequencies Under Modified Symmetry					
Independent	17.94	—	17.94	5.06	—	5.06
Republican/Democrat	9.36	11.70	21.06	2.64	3.30	5.94
Total	27.30	11.70	39.00	7.70	3.30	11.00

To specify a log-linear model for quasi-symmetry, we "flip" the entire K X K table over on its main diagonal, entering both this rotated table and the original table as a full three-dimensional array. Then the marginals fitted to the expanded data are {IJ}{IM}{JM} using our earlier notation of letting I represent the first (row) measure, J represent the second (column) measure, and M represent the two parts of the partition. The procedure is thus much like that in testing for symmetry except that the full table is used rather than the two triangular parts. The model that is fitted to the expanded data is also like the symmetry model though with the addition that the row and column totals are allowed to be different (through the inclusion of the {IM} and {JM} terms).

Since the first table is a duplicate of the second, the expected frequencies in both tables will duplicate each other, although in transposed order. Consequently, the L^2 must be divided in half, as should the df to obtain correct values for the test. Table 16 displays the expected frequencies for the quasi-symmetry hypothesis. An excellent fit is obtained, with $L^2 = .12$ and df equal to $(K - 1)(K - 2)/2 = 1$. Thus we conclude that the panel data approach symmetry, given unequal marginals in the two years. We are now (finally) in a position to test the hypothesis of marginal homogeneity. With the creation of the expected frequencies for the symmetry and quasi-symmetry models, we can obtain the L^2 for the hypothesis of marginal homogeneity by subtraction. The difference in L^2 between symmetry and

TABLE 16
Expected Frequencies Under the Quasi-Symmetry Model

1956 Party Identification	1960 Party Identification			Total
	Democrat	Independent	Republican	
Democrat	100.00	3.73	1.28	105
Independent	19.28	30.00	5.72	55
Republican	10.72	9.28	22.00	42
Total	130	43	29	202

quasi-symmetry models is 20.87 and the difference in df is 2. It is, therefore, reasonable to conclude that the marginal distribution of Catholic voter party identification differs significantly between 1956 and 1960.

Generalizations of marginal homogeneity, symmetry, and quasi-symmetry to three-dimensional data are possible (Bishop et al., 1975: 299-309). One of the more intriguing substantive applications was Hauser et al.'s (1975a, 1974b) demonstration that intergenerational occupational mobility in the United States has remained essentially constant despite marginal changes in the distribution of occupations between respondents and their fathers. Their method was to fit three-way log-linear models to two or more occupational mobility crosstabulations in which the parent-son association, {PS}, was hypothesized to be time-invariant (that is, $\tau_{ijk}^{PST} = 1.00$). Data from five large studies of U.S. men confirmed this hypothesis. The growing literature on log-linear applications to mobility includes recent articles by Hauser (1978), Goodman (1979d), and Duncan (1979).

Markov chain models. A special hypothesis which may be applied to categoric panel data of three or more waves is the test for a first-order Markov process, or a Markov chain analysis. Although we cover only the time stationarity hypothesis in Markov chains (explained below) as a natural extension of the previous section on two-wave panel data to the situation of three or more waves, the reader may, nevertheless, find this section dense without some prior elementary knowledge of Markov chains (see, e.g., Markus, 1979). When multiwave panel data are organized as square contingency tables with the starting state (response at time t) in the rows and the ending state (response at time t + 1) in the columns, the transition matrix (containing the probabilities that persons in any given state at time t will be in some particular state at time t + 1) can be estimated by forming the proportions within rows, that is

$$P_{ij} = f_{ij}/f_{i.}.$$

With data from at least three time points, there are two sets of transition probabilities: those from time 1 to time 2 and those from time 2 to time 3. Our first question of the data asks whether these two sets of transition probabilities are equal, that is, they have not changed over time (time stationarity hypothesis). If this hypothesis is supported by the data, it is possible to ask what will be the ultimate distribution of observations among categories after a long period of time. The question can be answered merely by raising the constant transition matrix to successively higher powers. Since the long-run marginal distribution is independent of the initial vector in a first-order stationary homogeneous Markov process, we speak of the flow of population among the states as ahistorical: The probability of a person's movement between states over time depends *only* upon the transition matrix (which is constant) and the state occupied immediately before the transition. It does not depend upon more temporally antecedent conditions.

To test for the time stationarity of the transition probabilities in a Markov chain, we require at minimum three observations on each individual, preferably at equally spaced intervals. Two crosstabulations are formed and stacked into a single three-way table. These matrices have the states occupied at the earlier observation period (F) in the rows and the states occupied at the next later observation time (S) in the columns with levels of the stack (T) corresponding to transition period. The cells of the table contain the observed frequencies. The log-linear model corresponding to the time stationarity of transition probabilities hypothesis (that ending state is a function of starting state but *not* of time) is:

$$F_{ijk} = \eta \; \tau_i^F \; \tau_j^S \; \tau_k^T \; \tau_{ij}^{FS} \; \tau_{ik}^{FT} . \qquad [28]$$

In other words, the model {FS}{FT} should provide an acceptable fit to the data if the stationarity hypothesis is correct. The {FT} term in the model has the same function as the requirement that the transition probabilities sum to 1.000 in each row (it makes the distribution of cases across starting states irrelevant to the model). But, given the starting state, F, the ending state, S, is independent of the time of transition, T, hence the τ_{jk}^{ST} term is not included in the model.

TABLE 17
Two One-Step Transition Matrices for Male Geographic Mobility

Origin Region	Destination Region				Total (N_i)
	Northeast	North-Central	South	West	
A. 1944-1951					
Northeast	.9645	.0087	.0122	.0145	1.000 (3437)
North-Central	.0048	.9575	.0120	.0257	1.000 (4160)
South	.0114	.0255	.9494	.0136	1.000 (4110)
West	.0082	.0291	.0157	.9475	1.000 (1341)
B. 1951-1953					
Northeast	.9803	.0047	.0091	.0059	1.000 (3393)
North-Central	.0022	.9750	.0082	.0147	1.000 (4157)
South	.0057	.0134	.9701	.0107	1.000 (4015)
West	.0013	.0088	.0067	.9831	1.000 (1483)

SOURCE: Spilerman, 1972.

Spilerman (1972) reported data from a study in 1958 which collected retrospective reports from males on their geographic movements for the previous 20 years. Two transition matrices from this study are shown in Table 17. Clearly, in the seven-year intervals covered by each wave, most men stayed in their initial regions, despite the great dislocations of World War II. But the observed values on the main diagonal are lower in the first matrix, suggesting that the geographic mobility process may not have remained constant over the full period. When the model in Equation 28 is fitted to the frequency crosstabulations corresponding to Table 17, $L^2 = 116.45$, df = 12. This significant departure from the model suggests that there is some nonstationarity in the transition probabilities over time. Of course, with more than 26,000 cases involved, finding an acceptable fit for anything less than the saturated model is difficult. If a plausible "baseline model" for evaluating the fit for a large sample is the set of three one-way marginals, {F}{S}{T}, which has $L^2 = 60,174$ for df = 24, then the stationarity hypothesis fares well, accounting for well over 99% of the variation in the two matrices. Our inclination is to reach the latter conclusion for that reason. For more advanced topics on Markov chains with categoric data, see Bishop et al. (1975: 257-279).

Age, period, and cohort models. In the study of social change, replicated cross-section studies have often been used to study the attitude and behavior patterns of cohorts of persons born at approximately the same historical time. Membership in a cohort is determined by the age of the respondent at the date (period) in which the survey was conducted. Thus, the three possible sources of variation (age, period, and cohort) in any dependent variables are not independent of each other:

$$\text{Cohort} = \text{Period} - \text{Age}. \qquad [29]$$

Any attempt to analyze dependent variables using all three "demographic" attributes as independent variables would result in an unidentified model whose effect parameters could not be uniquely estimated (Mason et al., 1973). The identification problem arises with categoric crosstabulations of data by age, period, and cohort just as it does with quantitative variables (Fienberg and Mason, 1979).

Recognition of the linear dependency between the three demographic variables has stimulated work to overcome the limitations of the identification problem. All such work begins by assuming additivity in the model such that all age effects are constant across periods and cohorts, that cohort effects are constant across age and period, and that period effects are constant across age and cohort. However, even with this assumption, identification problems remain. Recently, Fienberg and Mason (1979) proposed a logit model of the additive relationship between a dependent variable and age, period, and cohort measures which solved the technical problems of identification and estimation. A technical exposition of their solution is sufficiently complicated to prevent its full presentation here. However, a brief, nontechnical sketch of the approach suggests the protean nature of log-linear methodology for embracing the fundamental problems of social change.

Table 18 gives one possible display of some age-period-cohort data (from Smith, 1979), emphasizing age and period aspects. Entries on the same diagonal are in the same cohort. Note that the younger (8-11) and older (1-4) cohorts have missing observations for certain periods since their members had either not achieved age 15 or had exceeded age 49 (the age range covered) during the periods of time covered in the study.

To estimate expected frequencies for a table like Table 18, from which parameters for the three demographic variables (age, period and cohort) can be derived, an *identification specification* (Feinberg and Mason, 1979: 16) must be imposed (in addition to the assumption of additivity in the

TABLE 18
Age-Period-Cohort Crosstabulation of Homicide Frequencies per 100,000

	Period					
Age Group	1952-1956	1957-1961	1962-1967	1968-1971	1971-1976	Cohort
1. 15-19	6.2	7.5	8.6	15.1	17.1	11
2. 20-24	11.8	13.6	14.2	22.9	25.5	10
3. 25-29	12.4	11.9	13.6	19.3	22.2	9
4. 30-34	10.8	10.6	10.9	15.5	16.9	8
5. 35-39	9.4	8.8	9.1	12.5	13.4	7
6. 40-44	7.7	6.8	7.1	9.6	10.2	6
7. 45-49	6.1	5.7	5.5	7.3	7.4	
Cohort	1	2	3	4	5	

SOURCE: Smith, 1979.

model discussed earlier). That is, a restriction must be placed on one or more parameters to reduce the number of independent estimates which must be obtained. Examples include restrictions such that the effect of being in one age category is some particular constant ($\tau_1^A = c$), or that the effect of being in one cohort is equal to the effect of being in a second cohort ($\tau_1^C = \tau_2^C$). A single such restriction is sufficient to achieve identifiability so that all the parameters in the model can be estimated. The log-linear model {APC}{AD}{PD}{CD}—where A is age, P is period, C is cohort, and D is the dependent variable—can be used to estimate the desired expected cell frequencies by iterative proportional fitting. A brief outline of the procedure follows.

We begin by creating a new arrangement of the data in Table 18. (We have added the implied other half of the data: the frequency of non-homicides per 100,000. While we realize that the assumption of 100,000 cases per cell is unrealistic, this assumption does *not* influence the odds of a homicide which is the ultimate object of investigation.) This new arrangement is termed an unfolded table, and it consists of a four dimensional arrangement of Age × Period × Homicide. Because of space limitations, we have represented only a portion of the complete table in Table 19, but the general format can readily be seen. Each subtable is an age by period representation for a single cohort; all remaining cells in the subtable are structural zeros. For these data we have added an identification specification such that the effect of being age 40 to 44 is equal to the effect of being age 45 to 49. This is represented in the unfolded table by combining these two age groups (i.e., adding together the row for 40-44 and the row for 45-49).

The next step is to estimate the expected cell frequencies for the unfolded table as represented in Table 19, using the log-linear model {APC}{AH}{PH}{CH}—where A is age, P is period, C is cohort, and H is the dependent variable: homicide. Failure of the model to fit the data is an indication that there are nonadditive effects of age, period, and cohort, for example, that the age effects vary across periods or cohorts.

The expected frequencies for the data of Table 18 under the model {APC}{AH}{PH}{CH} were estimated and are given in Table 20. Table 21 provides goodness-of-fit data for this model and for other comparative models (on the simplified assumption of 100,000 cases in each cell of the original table). Relatively speaking, the additive model of age, period, and cohort effects (Model 8) reduces the L^2 from model 1 (no age, period, or cohort effects) by over 99%, indicating less than 1% of the variation as being the result of nonadditive effects of age, period, and cohort. It is also clear that the separate effects of age, period, and cohort overlap extensively. For example, whole cohort effects by themselves reduce the L^2 by 63%, cohort effects net of age and period account for only 6%.

To investigate the nature of the additive age, period, and cohort effects, effect parameters were calculated as follows using the expected odds of a homicide calculated by dividing the expected frequencies of homicides (Table 20) by the expected frequencies of nonhomicides (per 100,000). The procedure is not straightforward, and to understand it we first represent the odds (Ω or omega) in a cell as a function of effect parameters giving rise to the expected frequencies. Consider, for example, the expected odds for age group 6 (40-44), period 1, (1952-1956), which is part of cohort 2 as given in Equation 30.

$$\Omega_{612} = \frac{F_{6121}}{F_{6122}} = \frac{\eta \, \tau_{612}^{APC} \, \tau_{61}^{AH} \, \tau_{11}^{PH} \, \tau_{21}^{CH} \, \tau_6^{A} \, \tau_1^{P} \, \tau_2^{C} \, \tau_1^{H}}{\eta \, \tau_{612}^{APC} \, \tau_{62}^{AH} \, \tau_{12}^{PH} \, \tau_{22}^{CH} \, \tau_6^{A} \, \tau_1^{P} \, \tau_2^{C} \, \tau_2^{H}} \qquad [30]$$

TABLE 19

Partial Representation of the Four-Dimensional Array for Age-Period-Cohort and Homicide

		Homicide									
		Yes					No				
		Period					Period				
Cohort	Age	1952-1956	1957-1961	1962-1966	1967-1971	1972-1976	1952-1956	1957-1961	1962-1966	1967-1971	1972-1976
4	15-19	—*	—	—	—	—	—	—	—	—	—
	20-24	—	—	—	—	—	—	—	—	—	—
	25-29	—	—	—	—	—	—	—	—	—	—
	30-34	10.8	—	—	—	—	99989.2	—	—	—	—
	35-39	—	8.8	7.1	6.3	—	—	99991.2	99992.9	99993.7	—
	40-49	—	—	—	—	—	—	—	—	—	—
5	15-19	—	—	—	—	—	—	—	—	—	—
	20-24	—	—	—	—	—	—	—	—	—	—
	25-29	12.4	—	—	—	—	99987.6	—	—	—	—
	30-34	—	10.6	—	—	—	—	99989.4	—	—	—
	35-39	—	—	9.1	—	—	—	—	99990.9	—	—
	40-49	—	—	—	9.6	7.4	—	—	—	99990.4	99992.6

*Structural zero denoted by (—).

60

TABLE 20

Expected Frequencies for the Age-Period Cohort Data of Table 18, Under the Model {APC} {AH} {PH} {CH}

	Period					
Age Group	1952-1956	1957-1961	1962-1966	1967-1971	1972-1976	Cohort
1. 15-19	6.89	7.40	8.81	14.31	17.10	11
2. 20-24	12.04	12.91	14.18	22.58	26.29	10
3. 25-29	12.12	12.13	13.30	19.54	22.31	9
4. 30-34	10.53	10.62	10.86	15.92	16.78	8
5. 35-39	9.11	8.95	9.23	12.63	13.28	7
6. 40-44	7.62	7.09	7.12	9.82	9.64	6
7. 45-49	6.10	5.78	5.50	7.40	7.31	
Cohort	1	2	3	4	5	

TABLE 21

Models Fitted to Four-Way Crosstabulation of Age, Period, Cohort, and Homicide

Model	Fitted Marginals	L^2	d.f.
1	{APC}{H}	69.12	29
2	{APC}{AH}	29.42	24
3	{APC}{PH}	44.16	25
4	{APC}{CH}	25.74	20
5	{APC}{AH} {PH}	4.46	20
6	{APC}{AH} {CH}	3.12	15
7	{APC}{PH} {CH}	20.95	16
8	{APC}{AH} {PH} {CH}	0.30	12

Since all tau parameters not having to do with homicide (H) are the same in the numerator and the denominator they may be cancelled. Those tau parameters which do have to do with homicide in the numerator are the reciprocals of those in the denominator (cf. Equations 2 and 3), hence the whole ratio reduces to four products having to do with the age effect on homicide, the period effect on homicide, the cohort effect on homicide, and the marginal distribution of homicides:

$$\Omega_{612} = (\tau_{61}^{AH})^2 (\tau_{11}^{PH})^2 (\tau_{21}^{CH})^2 (\tau_1^{H})^2.$$ [31]

If we now construct the same ratio for age group 7, period 2, cohort 2, we have $\Omega_{722} = (\tau_{71}^{AH})^2 (\tau_{21}^{PH})^2 (\tau_{21}^{CH})^2 (\tau_1^{H})^2$. Finally, constructing a ratio of these two ratios (that is, the ratio of the expected odds for cell 6, 1, 2 to the expected odds for cell 7, 2, 2), we arrive at the following:

$$\frac{\Omega_{612}}{\Omega_{722}} = \frac{(\tau_{61}^{AH})^2 (\tau_{11}^{PH})^2 (\tau_{21}^{CH})^2 (\tau_1^{H})^2}{(\tau_{71}^{AH})^2 (\tau_{21}^{PH})^2 (\tau_{21}^{CH})^2 (\tau_1^{H})^2}.$$ [32]

Two terms in the numerator of Equation 32 are identical with two terms in the denominator and may be cancelled. With the identification restriction that the effect for age group 6 is equal to the effect for age group 7, this ratio further reduces to the square of the ratio of the effect for period 1 to the effect for period 2. Other ratios of expected odds yield similar ratios for the effects of period 2 relative to period 3, period 3 relative to 4, and so on. Finally, with the restriction that the product of the effects for all 5 periods must be unity (see Equation 23), we can solve for the magnitude of each of the effect parameters. In similar manner the effect parameters can now be calculated for age and cohort as well using both the ratios of expected odds from Table 20 and the earlier calculated effects for period. It might be wondered, since there are many cells in the table which could be used to calculate a ratio for say age group 4 to age group 5, which one should be used. The answer is that any of them may since they will all yield the same result (Feinberg and Mason, 1979: 14-15).

Table 22 presents the effect parameters for the additive age, period, cohort model. Briefly, it can be seen that period effects are decreasing over time, contrary to first impressions of Table 18. Age effects start low,

TABLE 22
Tau Parameters for the Model {APC} {AH} {PH} {CH}

Age		Period		Cohort	
τ_{11}^{AH}	0.701	τ_{11}^{PH}	1.232	τ_{11}^{CH}	0.547
τ_{21}^{AH}	1.028	τ_{21}^{PH}	1.073	τ_{21}^{CH}	0.612
τ_{31}^{AH}	1.105	τ_{31}^{PH}	0.945	τ_{31}^{CH}	0.677
τ_{41}^{AH}	1.109	τ_{41}^{PH}	0.964	τ_{41}^{CH}	0.771
τ_{51}^{AH}	1.094	τ_{51}^{PH}	0.831	τ_{51}^{CH}	0.888
τ_{61}^{AH}	1.034			τ_{61}^{CH}	1.019
τ_{71}^{AH}	1.034			τ_{71}^{CH}	1.163
				τ_{81}^{CH}	1.300
				τ_{91}^{CH}	1.501
				τ_{101}^{CH}	1.690
				τ_{111}^{CH}	1.651

peak in the 30-34 age category, and then diminish. Cohort effects, on the other hand, start very small and monotonically increase for each successive cohort save the last.

5. SPECIAL TECHNIQUES WITH LOG-LINEAR MODELS

Crosstabulations of social data sometime produce strange tables which cannot be subjected to log-linear analysis without some special modifications. This section considers a few of the more common problems which may arise.

A. What To Do About Zero Cells

The appearance of zeros in one or more cells can be a problem, since odds, odds ratios, and logits are undefined with zeros in the denominator.

Observed zero frequencies arise from two situations. Sampling zeros occur in finite samples, particularly when several variables are crosstabulated, due to the small probabilities for some categories (e.g., southern Jewish peanut farmers). The zero entry does not mean that such cases do not exist in the population, only that none fell into the sample. One virtue of log-linear models is that they can provide empirical estimates of the population frequencies despite the absence of empirical instances in the sample. The fitted model can generate nonzero expected frequencies (F_{ij}'s) despite observed zero frequencies (f_{ij}'s). Still, "too many" sampling zeros in the body of a table may create a problem where a marginal table to be fitted in the model contains zero cells. Two basic alternatives are possible: (1) add a small value to every cell in the body of the table, including those with nonzero frequencies. A value of .5 is often suggested (Goodman, 1970: 229). (This is a conservative procedure which will tend to underestimate effect parameters and their significance.) Or (2) arbitrarily define zero divided by zero to be zero (Fienberg, 1977: 109). In this second alternative, if any entry in a marginal table to be fitted in the model is zero, all entries giving rise to this zero will necessarily remain zero during iteration. An unlikely but possible third alternative would be to increase the sample size sufficiently to remove all zero cells.

The second situation producing observed zeros in the logical or fixed zero cell. Even if the entire population is available, certain classifications have no empirical referents. A logical zero may arise from a sampling design (omitting certain strata), an ordinal sequence of events (e.g., in an age by family status crosstabulation, cells for grandparents under the age of 25 will be empty), or a definitional inconsistency (e.g., no female can have a prostatectomy).

The log-linear solution to logical zeros is to define such cells as "structural zeros" (i.e., a consequence of the structure of the problem) and not to estimate the expected frequencies of such cells. In the previous section on two-wave panels we saw how log-linear models could be fitted to incomplete tables by fixing the structural zero cells in the starting values of the iteration procedure. The identical process is followed in testing the hypothesis of quasi-independence in a table with one or more structural zeros. Quasi-independence is a form of independence or nonassociation between variables when considering only that portion of the table containing nonzero entries. For example, in a two-way table, the quasi-independence model fits the log-linear equation

$$F_{ij} = \eta \, \tau_i^R \, \tau_j^C \qquad\qquad [33]$$

among that set of cells not designanted as logical zeros. The likelihood ratio chi-square is tested against a modified degree of freedom. If the table has I rows, J columns, and Z structural zero cells, the df's are (I–1) (J–1) – Z.

Table 23 illustrates the quasi-independence model with data on the sex-by-surgery crosstabulation. Certain types of operations are logically impossible for one of the sexes. The second panel shows the expected frequencies for the independence model when these logical zeros are ignored, while the third panel shows the expected frequencies when the logical cells are constrained to zero fixed values.

The standard independence model, which treats the empty cells as sampling zeros, estimates absurd values for female prostrate operations and male gynecological surgery. A poor fit is found with $L^2 = 622.52$, df = 13. When the quasi-independence model is fitted, not only are the two logical zero cells constrained but also the expected values of the remaining cells are much closer to the observed values, although the model still fails to adequately represent the data ($L^2 = 93.57$, df = 11). Clearly, surgical operations are differentially performed on males and females, leaving aside logically impossible procedures.

B. Fixing Start Values

Procedures for handling structural zero frequencies in incomplete tables involve setting the start values for the Iterative Proportional Fitting algorithm to zero in the appropriate cells. In other instances, we may wish to constrain certain cells to the observed frequencies, estimating various log-linear models on the remaining cells. Again, such models require setting some values in the ECTA starting table to a priori values before beginning the iterative fitting. A case in point concerns the analysis of intergenerational occupational mobility, for example, data obtained from Blau and Duncan's (1967) classic study and shown in Table 24. It is clear from the second panel that the usual model of independence between rows and columns does not fit at all well. The five main diagonal cells are grossly underestimated, reflecting a tendency of many men to remain in the broad category of origin. (This model $L^2 = 830.98$, df = 16.)

An alternative model, first proposed by Goodman (1965), is quasi-perfect mobility. In this model the main diagonal entries are fixed to their observed values, and the off-diagonal entries are estimated as in a model of quasi-independence. Procedurally, the main diagonal values are entered and treated as structural zeros; the marginal tables {P} {S}, are

TABLE 23
Crosstabulation of Sex and Surgical Operation (ten thousands)

Surgical Operation	Observed Values		Independence H_0		Quasi-Independence H_0	
	Male	Female	Male	Female	Male	Female
Neurosurgery	18	20	16.2	21.8	19.9	18.1
Ophthalmology	33	44	32.7	44.3	40.3	36.7
Otorhinolarynology	175	89	112.3	151.8	138.3	125.7
Vascular-Cardiac	59	38	41.2	55.8	50.8	46.2
Thoracic	16	12	11.9	16.1	14.7	13.3
Abdominal	139	142	119.5	161.5	147.2	133.8
Urological	86	45	55.7	75.3	68.6	62.4
Prostatectomy	27	—	11.5	15.5	27.0	—
Breast	2	36	16.2	21.8	19.9	18.1
Gynecological	—	383	162.9	220.2	—	383.0
Orthopedic	135	129	112.3	151.8	138.3	125.7
Plastic	55	53	45.9	62.1	56.6	51.4
Oral-Dental	26	30	23.8	32.2	29.3	26.7
Biopsy	39	74	48.1	65.0	59.2	53.8
Total	810	1,095	810	1,095	810	1,095

SOURCE: Ranofsky, 1978.

fitted; df's are reduced by five because the diagonal values have been fixed. The main diagonal values are then reinserted in the display (Table 24 C). Quasi-perfect mobility remarkably improves the fit, as the third panel of Table 24 shows. The L^2 is now 255.14, a reduction of 575.84 at the cost of only five degrees of freedom.

A further improvement in fit can be achieved by dividing the 20 non-diagonal cells into two sets of ten, corresponding to men with upward and downward mobility relative to their fathers' occupations. Each of these triangular subtables can be tested for quasi-independence by methods used in the previous section. For example, in testing the down-wardly mobile half of the table, we assume structural zeros along the main diagonal and in the lower triangular section of the table. The expected frequencies are shown in the fourth panel of Table 24. The upwardly mobile subset yields $L^2 = 28.97$ for df = 3, while the downwardly mobile subset has $L^2 = 3.63$, also for df = 3. The combined $L^2 = 32.60$, df = 6 indicates that while the model still differs from the data significantly, a remarkable improvement over the original standard independence model has been made, even with the large sample size (3396 tens of thousands, i.e., 33,960,000).

TABLE 24
Intergenerational Occupational Mobility of White American Men
(ten thousands)

Fathers' Occupations	Sons' Occupations				
	Professional & Managerial	Clerical & Sales	Craftsmen	Operatives & Laborers	Farmers
A. Observed Frequencies					
Prof. & Manag.	152	66	33	39	4
Clerical-Sales	201	159	72	80	8
Craftsmen	138	125	184	172	7
Ops. & Labor.	143	161	209	378	17
Farmers	98	146	207	371	226
B. Expected Frequencies, Standard Independence Model					
Prof. & Manag.	63.4	56.9	61.0	90.0	22.7
Clerical-Sales	112.1	100.6	108.0	159.3	40.1
Craftsmen	134.9	121.1	130.0	191.7	48.3
Ops. & Labor.	195.7	175.7	188.5	278.1	70.1
Farmers	225.9	202.8	217.6	320.9	80.9
C. Expected Frequencies, Quasi-Perfect Mobility Model					
Prof. & Manag.	152	38.1	41.9	58.7	3.3
Clerical-Sales	99.9	159	105.4	147.5	8.2
Craftsmen	125.7	120.4	184	185.5	10.4
Ops. & Labor.	171.3	164.1	180.6	378	14.1
Farmers	183.1	175.4	193.1	270.3	226
D. Expected Frequencies, Modified Quasi-Perfect Model					
Prof. & Manag.	152	66.0	33.8	39.6	2.6
Clerical-Sales	201.0	159	71.2	83.3	5.4
Craftsmen	122.9	140.1	184	168.0	11.0
Ops. & Labor.	124.7	142.1	246.3	378	17.0
Farmers	131.5	149.8	259.7	371.0	226

SOURCE: Blau and Duncan, 1967: 496.

C. Analyzing Ordered Data

All the models we have considered to this point make no assumptions about the order of the variable categories. The L^2 tests for fit are insensitive to the order in which categories occur; it remains unchanged upon permu-

TABLE 25
Crosstabulation of Age, Religion, and Church Attendance

Religion	Age	Church Attendance			Odds	
		Low	Medium	High	Medium:Low	High:Low
		A. Observed Frequencies				
Non-Catholic	Young	322	124	141	0.39	0.44
Non-Catholic	Old	250	152	194	0.61	0.78
Catholic	Young	88	45	106	0.51	1.20
Catholic	Old	28	24	119	0.86	4.25
		B. Expected Frequencies				
Non-Catholic	Young	329.05	127.90	130.05	0.39	0.40
Non-Catholic	Old	242.95	148.10	204.95	0.61	0.84
Catholic	Young	80.95	41.10	116.95	0.51	1.44
Catholic	Old	35.05	27.90	108.05	0.80	3.08
		Expected Odds Ratios			Observed Odds Ratios	
Non-Catholic	Young	1	1	1	1	1	1
Non-Catholic	Old	1	1.56	2.10	1	1.56	1.77
Catholic	Young	1	1.31	3.60	1	1.31	2.73
Catholic	Old	1	2.05	7.70	1	2.21	9.66

tation of rows and columns. If the researcher is interested in testing whether one of the variables in a table in fact has ordinal properties, log-linear models may be modified to provide such tests. Simon (1974) shows how an iterative procedure can estimate expected cell frequencies in a two-way table in which the column categories are assigned scores (for example, 1, 2, 3, 4 for a four-category variable). Fienberg (1975: 52-58) also discusses this procedure and how it may be generalized to three or more dimensions and include quadratic or higher order components as well as ordinal properties for more than one variable.

In our illustration, we follow a technique described by Duncan (1979) in which a trichotomous dependent variable in a three-way table is scaled. Table 25 gives the observed frequencies for the 1972 General Social Survey crosstabulation of age, religion, and church attendance, as well as the odds and odds ratios for the fitted model {AR}{AC}{RC} (L^2 = 7.25, df = 2). If the four-by-three table of expected odds ratios at the bottom of Table 25 is used as a set of starting values in fitting model {AR}{C}, it will exactly reproduce the expected frequencies generated by the model {AR}{AC}

{RC}. However, there is no gain in df, since from the six df's associated with the first model we must subtract the four df's used to calculate the expected odds ratios (although six odds ratios are shown, two are redundant; prove this to yourself). The reason that using the expected odds ratio as starting values in fitting the model {AR}{C} will reproduce the expected frequencies generated by the model {AR}{AC}{RC} is that the iterative proportional fitting alogorithm does not change the odds ratios given in the starting values *except* for those involved in the marginals being fit. By using start values which incorporate the desired odds ratios for the (AC) and (RC) relationships and then fitting the model {AR}{C} which does not alter the built-in (AC) and (RC) relationships, we end up with a model equivalent to {AR}{AC}{CR}.

We can use this procedure, however, in other ways. Rather than trying to reproduce the normal unconstrained (AC)(RC) relationships as suggested above, these relationships could be constrained to a particular form (linear, quadratic, linear in the logarithmic scale, and so on) through appropriate choice of starting values to reflect odds of this form.

For example, suppose that instead of four independent odds ratios we design a set of starting values with the form:

$$
\begin{array}{ccc}
1 & 1 & 1 \\
1 & c & c^2 \\
1 & y & y^2 \\
1 & cy & c^2y^2
\end{array}
$$

where there are now only two parameters to be estimated and the odds of medium:low and high:low attendance to age and religion will be constrained to linearity in the logarithmic scale. Obtaining numerical values for c and y is a tedious trial and error process of inserting different values in the starting table until the L^2 for one pair reaches a minimum. (Duncan, 1979, shows how the Simon technique for a two-way table may be used to identify upper and lower bounds on the values of c and y with which to begin the search.)

For the data in Table 20 we found the following starting values for odds ratios gave the lowest $L^2 = 14.62$, df = 4:

1	1	1
1	1.47	2.16
1	1.94	3.76
1	2.85	8.13

where c = 1.47 and y = 1.94. These expected odds ratios under the linear constraints model can be compared with the observed values in Table 25. A fairly consistent overestimate is obvious in all but two cases. Figure 3 gives an idea of the difference between the observed and the fitted odds ratios for the linear constraints model. These ratios are calculated on the independent variables within categories of church attendance. The linear constraints fitted by the starting values require the two lines to be parallel. Duncan (1979) shows how this requirement can be relaxed to retain linearity while permitting the lines to diverge (i.e., have different slopes).

D. Collapsing Polytomous Variables

Frequently analysts of crosstabulations collapse the categories of polytomous variables prior to analysis either to simplify the interpretation or to avoid the problems of sampling zeros noted above. Yet, too often such collapsing is done on an ad hoc basis, combining categories adjacent to each other or with small marginal frequencies. A method for testing the collapsibility of a polytomous variable in the crosstabulation context was developed by Duncan (1975) and is illustrated here with the three-way data in Table 26. The dependent variable was agreement or disagreement with an item asking whether a woman should be allowed to have a legal abortion because she was too poor to support more children. The odds of favorable to unfavorable response differ noticeably between some of the four religious groups, although relatively little change occurred over the six years. Fitting various three-way logit models to the data confirms this perception, with the fitted marginals {RY}{RA} being adequate to

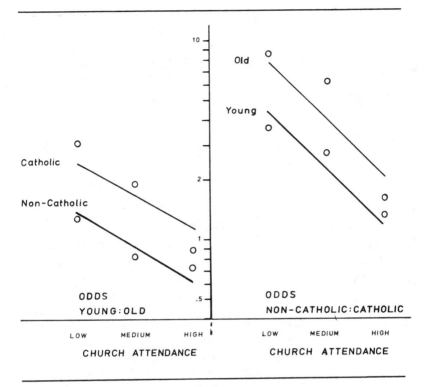

Figure 3: Observed and Expected Log Ratios

represent the data (L^2 = 1.89, df = 4). In contrast, the logit model in which abortion attitude depends on neither independent variable, {RY}{A}, fits the data extremely poorly (L^2 = 130.16, df = 6).

The question we can ask next is whether the four-category religion variable is collapsible into three or fewer categories, producing a model intermediate between the two above which gives a parsimonious accounting of the data. To set up the test, the religion variable is replaced by four dichotomous variables—Protestant (P), Catholic (C), Jew (J), and Other (O)—which are effect coded as shown in Table 27. This procedure is thus similar to the use of dummy variables in regression analysis. Structural zeros are specified in the starting table for those combinations of the dichotomous variables which are illogical (i.e., respondent occupies more than one religious category). The corresponding models to the two investigated above are {YPCJO}{A} and {YPCJO}{PCJOA}. But we can now test a variety of intermediate models, in which some of the religious vari-

TABLE 26
Crosstabulation of Abortion Attitude by Religion and Time

Religion	1972 Attitude		1978 Attitude		Odds on Favorable	
	Favor	Oppose	Favor	Oppose	1972	1978
Protestant	460	498	424	501	.92	.85
Catholic	147	240	151	225	.61	.67
Jew	41	10	23	6	4.10	3.83
Other	65	17	88	30	3.82	2.93

ables but not others are allowed to affect abortion attitude. The results of these analyses are shown in Table 28. Each of the intermediate models (2-11 in the table) shows the results of collapsing various categories of the religion variable. For example, model {YPCJO}{CA} has only an effect for being Catholic or non-Catholic on attitudes toward abortion. The other religious categories are by implication collapsed together and have no separate effects. The best fitting model, 11, has separate effects for being Catholic or non-Catholic and for being Protestant or non-Protestant. The categories of Jewish and Other have no separate effects and are implicitly grouped or collapsed together. The result is a religious trichotomy. The expected frequencies under this model are also shown in Table 27. The odds on a favorable response are identical in both years: .89 for Protestants, .64 for Catholics, and 3.44 for Jews and Others.

E. Nonhierarchical Models

We have indicated in a number of places that we were restricting ourselves to a consideration of hierarchical models, and indeed we believe that this restriction makes sense in most applications, for reasons we shall point out. It was the case, however, when Goodman first started presenting his work on log-linear models, which included this restriction to hierarchical models, many people reacted by feeling that was too constraining; they wanted to investigate nonhierarchical models (probably only because they believed they could not). Actually, the restriction to hierarchical models in not a characteristic of log-linear models, but a characteristic of the Iterative Proportional Fitting algorithm for estimating the expected frequencies in the log-linear models. Other algorithms—such as the Newton-Raphson algorithm which is incorporated into Bock and Yates program MULTIQUAL or Haberman's program FREQ, for example—do not have this restriction.

TABLE 27
Effect Coding and Expected Frequencies for Collapsing
Religion in Table 26

Dichotomous Religion Variables				1972 Attitude		1978 Attitude	
Protestant	Catholic	Jew	Other	Favor	Against	Favor	Against
1	1	1	1	—	—	—	—
1	1	1	0	—	—	—	—
1	1	0	1	—	—	—	—
1	1	0	0	—	—	—	—
1	0	1	1	—	—	—	—
1	0	1	0	—	—	—	—
1	0	0	1	—	—	—	—
1	0	0	0	449.75	508.25	434.26	490.74
0	1	1	1	—	—	—	—
0	1	1	0	—	—	—	—
0	1	0	1	—	—	—	—
0	1	0	0	151.15	235.85	146.85	229.15
0	0	1	1	—	—	—	—
0	0	1	0	39.52	11.48	22.47	6.53
0	0	0	1	63.55	18.45	91.45	26.55
0	0	0	0	—	—	—	—

TABLE 28
Log-Linear Models for Collapsibility of Religion in Table 23

Model	Fitted Marginals	L^2	d.f.	p
1	{YPCJO} {A}	130.16	6	.00
2	{YPCJO} {PA}	128.57	5	.00
3	{YPCJO} {CA}	98.21	5	.00
4	{YPCJO} {JA}	94.03	5	.00
5	{YPCJO} {OA}	56.49	5	.00
6	{YPCJO} {PA} {JA}	94.03	4	.00
7	{YPCJO} {JA} {CA}	68.04	4	.00
8	{YPCJO} {OA} {PA}	52.72	4	.00
9	{YPCJO} {OA} {CA}	37.47	4	.00
10	{YPCJO} {OA} {JA}	15.65	4	.00
11	{YPCJO} {CA} {PA}	2.30	4	$>$.50
12	{YPCJO} {PCJOA}	1.89	3	$>$.50

Why does the restriction to hierarchical models make sense in most applications? To see the answer let us consider again the four-variable crosstabulation we discussed when we first introduced the idea of hierarchical models: Vote Turnout (V), Education (E), Race (R), and Voluntary Association Memberships (M). Ignoring education for the moment, let us consider the model {VMR}. If this model fit the data, it would indicate that the effect of membership on voter turnout varied by race. The full hierarchical model would be:

$$F_{ijk} = \eta \tau_i^V \, \tau_j^M \, \tau_k^R \, \tau_{ij}^{VM} \, \tau_{ik}^{VR} \, \tau_{jk}^{MR} \, \tau_{ijk}^{VMR} \; .$$

Now let us consider a nonhierarchical alternative to this model as follows:

$$F_{ijk} = \eta \tau_i^V \, \tau_j^M \, \tau_k^R \, \tau_{ij}^{VM} \, \tau_{jk}^{MR} \, \tau_{ijk}^{VMR} \; .$$

In this nonhierarchical alternative we have left out the vote X race term. Actually, such a model does not leave out the term, rather it assumes that the effect is nonexistent (i.e., that the value of the tau parameter is 1.00). Since an interaction effect involving all three terms is present in the model, however, and since our earlier interpretation of this effect as indicating that the membership-voter turnout relationship varied by race is not the only interpretation, we must look carefully to see what our nonhierarchical model implies. First, consider another valid interpretation of the three way effect: that the relationship between race and voter turnout varies by voluntary association membership. In our nonhierarchical model, however, we assume that there is no relationship between race and voter turnout. For this to be the case, and for there to be a significant three-way effect, it must be the case that the race-turnout relationship among those with no memberships is equal in magnitude but opposite in direction to the same relationship among those with one or more voluntary association memberships, and together these two partial relationships exactly cancel each other out. Is this a reasonable a priori assumption? In most situations the answer is obviously no, and it is for this reason that in most situations nonhierarchical models do not make sense.

In some situations, however, nonhierarchical models do make sense, and for illustrative purposes we consider one briefly. For this example we reconsider our data illustrating comparative cross-section analysis (page 47). We were looking there at the question of whether the relationship between party (P) and presidential vote (V) varied over time (T; between 1972 and 1976) and we concluded that it did not since the model {TP}

TABLE 29
Tau Parameters for the Hierarchical and Nonhierarchical
Version of $\{TP\}\{TV\}\{PV\}$

	Model	
Parameters	Hierarchical	Nonhierarchical
τ_1^T	0.99	(1.00)
τ_1^P	1.54	1.52
τ_2^P	1.12	1.12
τ_1^V	0.76	0.76
τ_{11}^{TP}	1.11	1.09
τ_{12}^{TP}	1.05	1.05
τ_{11}^{TV}	0.81	0.81
τ_{11}^{PV}	2.44	2.44
τ_{21}^{PV}	1.08	1.09
L^2	1.88	2.09
df	2	3
p	.39	.55

$\{TV\}\{PV\}$ adequately fit the data. This hierarchical model may be written out in full as

$$F_{ijk} = \eta \tau_i^T \ \tau_j^P \ \tau_k^V \ \tau_{ij}^{TP} \ \tau_{ik}^{TV} \ \tau_{jk}^{PV} \ .$$

Because the analysis draws on two cross-sectional samples of (nearly) the same size, one can make the a priori assumption that the value of τ^T is unity, that is, has no effect. Incorporating this assumption, the following nonhierarchical model was estimated

$$F_{ijk} = \eta \tau_j^P \ \tau_k^V \ \tau_{ij}^{TP} \ \tau_{ik}^{TV} \ \tau_{jk}^{PV} \ .$$

Table 29 presents the results of this analysis compared with the results of the earlier analysis. As can be seen, the effect parameters change very little and the value of L^2 changes very little. There is an increase of one degree of freedom since one fewer parameter is being estimated.

6. CONCLUSIONS

This introduction to log-linear models for contingency table analysis just scratches the surface of potential adaptations and applications. The place of these methods in the social sciences becomes more secure with each passing year.

Two rival techniques for the systematic quantitative analysis of cross-tabulations have come into prominence and deserve a brief comment in conclusion. Davis (1975) proposed a system of linear flow graphs and corresponding equations (d-systems). Closely related to ordinary least-squares regression, d-systems analysis was designed explicitly for causal modelling of small systems of categoric variables. The effects of antecedent causes on dependent variables are expressed in terms of changes in proportions (hence, d for difference) rather than odds. Davis argued that his approach copes with interactions in a parallel fashion but has certain advantages over log-linear models in depicting causal transmittance through intervening variables.

The second technique, which has gained greater popularity with political scientists than among sociologists, is the minimum logit chi-square method developed by Grizzle et al. (1969; see also Kritzer, 1978). The dependent variable to be explained is the probability of a particular response (outcome). Main effects and interactions are specified in a model through manipulation of a design matrix of effect-coded dummy variables. This process enables the researcher to construct and estimate nonhierarchical models. While the G-S-K approach has an advantage over log-linear methods in the greater familiarity of most users with probability interpretations of categoric data, the handling of zero (empty) cells appears more problematic.

The choice of data analysis techniques ultimately should be based upon the substantive formulation of research problems, rather than an arbitrary injunction that single method should be invoked for all contingencies. If the present exposition has moved the reader toward a better grasp of one particular method, we have achieved our aim.

REFERENCES

ASHER, H. B. (1976) Causal Modelling. Beverly Hills, CA: Sage.

BISHOP, Y.M.M. and S. E. FIENBERG (1969) "Incomplete two-dimensional contingency tables." Biometrica 22: 119-128.

——— and P. W. HOLLAND (1975) Discrete Multivariate Analysis: Theory and Practice. Cambridge: MIT Press.

BOCK, R. D. and G. YATES (1973) "MULTIQUAL, loglinear analysis of nominal and ordinal qualitative data by the method of maximum likelihood: A FORTRAN program." Chicago: National Educational Resources.

BLAU, P. M. and O. D. DUNCAN (1967) The American Occupational Structure. New York: John Wiley.

DAVIS, J. A. (1976) "Analyzing contingency tables with linear flow graphs: D systems." Pp. 111-145 in D. R. Heise (ed.), Sociological Methodology 1976. San Francisco: Jossey-Bass.

——— (1974) "Hierarchical models for significance tests in multivariate contingency tables: an exegesis of Goodman's recent papers." Pp. 189-231 in H. L. Costner (ed.), Sociological Methodology 1973-1974. San Francisco: Jossey-Bass.

DUNCAN, O. D. (1980) "Testing key hypotheses in panel analysis." Pp. 279-289 K. F. Schuessler (ed.), Sociological Methodology 1981. San Francisco: Jossey-Bass.

——— (1979) "How destination depends on origin in the occupational mobility table." American Journal of Sociology 84: 793-803.

——— (1975a) Introduction to Structural Equation Models. New York: Academic Press.

——— (1975b) "Partitioning polytomous variables in multiway contingency analysis." Social Science Research 4: 167-182.

——— (1966) "Path analysis: sociological examples." American Journal of Sociology 72: 1-16.

——— and J. A. McRAE, Jr. (1978) "Multiway contingency analysis with a scaled response or factor." Pp. 68-85 in K. F. Schuessler (ed.), Sociological Methodology 1980. San Francisco: Jossey-Bass.

FIENBERG, S. E. (1977) The Analysis of Cross-Classified Data. Cambridge: MIT Press.

——— and W. M. MASON (1978) "Identification and estimation of age-period-cohort models in the analysis of discrete archival data." Pp. 1-67 in K. F. Schuessler (ed.), Sociological Methodology 1980. San Francisco: Jossey-Bass.

78

GOODMAN, L. A. (1979a) "A brief guide to the causal analysis of data from surveys." American Journal of Sociology 84: 1078-1095.
—— (1979b) "Multiplicative models for square contingency tables with ordered categories." Biometrika 66: 413-418.
—— (1979c) "Simple models for the analysis of association in cross-classifications having ordered categories." Journal of the American Statistical Association 74: 537-552.
—— (1979d) "Multiplicative models for the analysis of occupational mobility tables and other kinds of cross-classification tables." American Journal of Sociology 84: 804-819.
—— (1973a) "Causal analysis of data from panel studies and other kinds of surveys." American Journal of Sociology 78: 1135-1191.
—— (1973b) "The analysis of multidimensional contingency tables when some variables are posterior to others: a modified path analysis approach." Biometrika 60: 178-192.
—— (1972a) "A modified multiple regression approach to the analysis of dichotomous variables." American Sociological Review 37: 28-46.
—— (1972b) "A general model for the analysis of surveys." American Journal of Sociology 77: 1035-1086.
—— (1970) "The multivariate analysis of qualitative data: interactions among multiple classifications." Journal of the American Statistical Association 65: 226-256.
—— (1965) "On the statistical analysis of mobility tables." American Journal of Sociology 70: 564-585.
GRIZZLE, J. E., C. F. STARMER, and G. G. KOCH (1969) "Analysis of categorical data by linear models." Biometrics 25: 489-504.
HABERMAN, S. J. (1979) Analysis of Qualitative Data (Vol. 2). New York: Academic Press.
—— (1978) Analysis of Qualitative Data (Vol. 1). New York: Academic Press.
HAUSER, R. M. (1978) "A structural model of the mobility table." Social Forces 56: 919-953.
—— J. N. KOFFEL, H. P. TRAVIS, and P. J. DICKINSON (1975a) "Temporal change in occupational mobility: Evidence for men in the United States." American Sociological Review 40: 279-297.
—— (1975b) "Structural changes in occupational mobility among men in the United States." American Sociological Review 40: 585-598.
JORESKOG, K. G. (1970) "A general method for analysis of covariance structures." Biometrika 57: 239-251.
KNOKE, D. (1976) Change and Continuity in American Politics: The Social Bases of Politics. Baltimore: Johns Hopkins University Press.
—— and R. THOMSON (1977) "Voluntary association membership trends and the family life cycle." Social Forces 56: 48-65.
KRITZER, H. M. (1978) "An introduction to multivariate contingency table analysis." American Journal of Political Science 22: 187-226.
MARKUS, G. B. (1979) Analyzing Panel Data. Beverly Hills, CA: Sage.
MASON, K. O., W. M. MASON, H. H. WINSBOROUGH, and W. K. POOLE (1973) "Some methodological issues in cohort analysis of archival data." American Sociological Review 38: 242-258.
McNEMAR, Q. (1962) Psychological Statistics. New York: John Wiley.
OLSEN, M. (1972) "Social participation and voting turnout: a multivariate analysis." American Sociological Review 37: 317-333.
RANOFSKY, A. L. (1978) Utilization of Short-Stay Hospitals: Annual Summary of the United States, 1976 (Vital and Health Statistics Series 13 No. 37). Hyattsville, MD: National Center for Health Statistics.
REYNOLDS, H. T. (1977) Analysis of Nominal Data. Beverly Hills, CA: Sage.

SIMON, G. (1974) "Alternative analyses for the singly-ordered contingency table." Journal of the American Statistical Association 69: 971-976.

SMITH, M. D. (1979) "Increases in youth violence: age, period or cohort effect." Presented at the meetings of the American Sociological Association, Boston.

SPILERMAN, S. (1972) "The analysis of mobility processes by the introduction of independent variables into a Markov chain." American Sociological Review 37: 277-294.

STEPHAN, F. and P. McCARTHY (1958) Sampling Opinions. New York: John Wiley.

THOMSON, R. and D. KNOKE (1980) "Voluntary associations and voting turnout of American ethnoreligious groups." Ethnicity (forthcoming).

VERBA, S. and N. H. NIE (1972) Participation in America: Political Democracy and Social Equality. New York: Harper & Row.

DAVID KNOKE is Associate Professor of Sociology at Indiana University. He was awarded a National Institute of Mental Health research scientist development award to work on problems of voluntary associations. His most recent book (coauthored with James R. Wood) is Organized for Action: Commitment in Voluntary Associations *(Rutgers University Press, forthcoming).*

PETER J. BURKE is Professor of Sociology and Department Chairman at Indiana University. His current work concerns two related (he thinks) issues: understanding the structure of the self and understanding the structure of talk in small group interaction.